The Cheetahs 1976 – The Resurrection

by Keith Lawson

*Better
Than
Nothing*

The Cheetahs 1976 – The Resurrection

Published by Better Than Nothing, Poole, Dorset, UK.

First published 2018

Printed by lulu.com

Copyright © Keith Lawson 2018

ISBN: 978-0-244-69934-5

"Last season I looked at the Oxford track and firmly believed that I'd seen the last of speedway at Cowley. The news that Bristol Stadiums had sold out was not really a surprise, but the speed of the deal seemed almost indecent.

As the Dunton/Dugard regime made plans to move, first to Harringay and subsequently White City there seemed little hope. Pete Jarman's training school kept the place alive, but only just. But happily everyone reckoned without a big hearted bunch of local enthusiasts and three men who cared about the future of Oxford Speedway.

I remember my good friend Roger Jones telling me in confidence that 1975 Stoke promoters, Harry Bastable and Tony Allsopp, had been in touch and hoped to bring the team into the New National League. So Harry and Tony, who I knew from my connections with Birmingham where they are regular and welcome spectators, joined forces with the SOS Committee, kept Roger on as manager and kept speedway alive. And I must say, when I looked in at a pre-season practice, I was amazed. The sheer hard work and dedication of the volunteers had made the stadium look better than I'd ever seen it."

Bob Radford 1976

"May we welcome you all to what we hope is going to be a highly successful season for the New Oxford Cheetahs. To those who have never sampled National League Speedway we believe that you are in for more than a few pleasant surprises, and at the end of the evening we feel sure that you will have adopted your own personal favourite from our super seven.

During the winter it appeared inevitable that speedway was lost to Oxford for the 1976 season, but the sterling work put in by the S.O.S Committee, Dave Clinkard, and the "paint brush brigade" turned the tables in favour of the happy position which we have today."

Harry Bastable's and Tony Allsopp's message in the very first programme 1976

FOREWORD

There is a lot of nostalgia for me in this book. It records the resurrection of the Oxford Cheetahs at Cowley Stadium after a closed season when we thought we would never see speedway at Sandy Lane again.

I am proud to have served on the SOS Committee (with other wonderful people) and we were able to get a reprieve and hear the sound of bikes around the arena once more. The Cheetahs went on to glory but, sadly, yet again the stadium sits silent and fans hope and pray for a miracle.

So, to commemorate a landmark year, I have taken my photos (in whatever condition they have been rescued from poor storage) from my time as Trackside Photographer, added the data of results and scorecard (with grateful thanks to Steve Wilkes and Gary Done for their research and tireless efforts) and any stories I can remember or people have told me.

And I cannot promise this is a definitive record – it is what it is. So enjoy, please, what is here and not what is missing. And where you find a gap, make it your project to complete.

To my heroes and friends of 1976, I dedicate this book.6

While preparing this book, the sad news that the speedway world had lost Bob Dugard reached me. Although I primarily reported to Danny Dunton during the period of Oxford Rebels, my contact with Bob was always friendly and respectful. I am sorry he has been taken from us.

BEHIND THE SCENES (1976 – the 28th season)

Those who performed to maintain the standards and safety for the enjoyment of the fans (in no particular order, with some omissions)

Tom Prickett (Starting marshal)

Dave Hammond (Announcer)

Dr T Faulkner (Medical Officer)

Bernard Crapper (Clerk of the Course)

John Hancox (Pit Marshal and Machine Examiner)

C. Constance (Colour Marshall)

M. Pearson (SCB Timekeeper)

George Squires, Bill Spicer

and the Track Maintenance guys

and the St John's Ambulance volunteers, led by Supt. Bill Tombs

THE SUPPORTERS' CLUB OFFICIALS
(who stayed with Oxford and rebuilt the Club)

Dave Clinkard

John Payne

Ann Cross

Dave Clinkard

and the countless unnamed fans who supported the SOS campaign, who turned up at public meetings, who came to paint and clean, and who paid at the turnstiles to keep the speedway running. You are all owed a debt by the fans who would come later and see the Cheetahs rise to such success.

THE STORY

Even before the end of the 1975 season, it was known that the Stadium was under threat from closure as Bristol Stadiums withdrew instead of renewing a lease. From among the fans and the greyhound community, a Save Our Stadium committee was formed:

Bernard Crapper

Dave Clinkard

Mick Harris

Peter Jones

Les Windle

Tony West

George Squires

A. Baker

Lynn Dooley

Keith Lawson (myself)

with support from Liberal councillor, Margaret Butler (who kindly hosted some meetings at her home).

We lobbied, attended council meetings, had public meetings and the amount of support for the stadium to continue was finally recognised and a lease offered. Then came the second problem, how to pay for it.

The speedway fans might have been the most vocal but it was from greyhound fans that the finances were provided. A further bill came when it was realised the that the Totaliser (essential for greyhound racing) had to be rented and other fixtures were not included in the sale to the Council (who had only been interested in the land for development)

We got the green light and fans turned up to decorate the stadium. Eve Cavender persuaded her boss at Manders to donate the paint. Mick Harris took charge of the stock and as people arrived and asked "What can I do?" I said go and see the foreman – and the name stuck.

Radio Oxford turned up to broadcast live.

Despite my fear of heights, I used a flat bed truck with a ladder on the bed to reach the bridge over the pit tunnel to repaint the cheetahs.

Dave Clinkard organised a caravan into the Pits for Steve Holden and Cliff Anderson to live in. It took some cleaning up and we papered the walls with pages from the Speedway Star and photos.

7

Cliff would use the workshop to tune engines (he looked after Ole Olsen's bikes) and both of them would do track maintenance and put up the ply boards for race nights and take then down for the greyhound racing.

Steve also did DJ work in the Clubhouse. Tony Dell was brought in as Entertainments Officer and moved into the White Buffalo, the big house next door to the stadium, with his wife. Steve, Cliff and I used to hang around with Tony on other projects – one was to try and get TV work as stunt riders, as Tony had already worked in that field. Sadly that never happened but we did have fun promoting ourselves. If only I could find the photos we did for promoting ourselves... but no, lost!

Eric Morecambe and Tony Dell 1976.

Working alongside Tony introduced me to the girl who would become my
wife (and is still with me).

The Supporters Club had split- some opting to continue with the Rebels at White City and others, like Dave Clinkard and Ann Cross, loyal to Oxford. There was some acrimony over the Club's funds – one argument was that the pot had been raised for the Rebels and the counter argument that it belonged to the fans who still supported Oxford, which was, I believe, the winning argument.

Of course, we needed promoters and we were lucky that Harry Bastable and Tony Allsopp had a licence but no stadium. Harry asked me if there were someone who could be Clerk of the Course and the obvious choice was Bernard Crapper. The rest, as they say, is history. A good man, Bernard, a personal friend, and taken from us far too soon.

When discussing a name for the new team, I made the suggestion to Harry and Tony that the obvious choice was The Cheetahs, as the name would resonate with the fans and the history of Sandy Lane. In "The Story of Oxford Speedway", the authors Robert Bamford and Glynn Shailes would say "Reverting to the old nickname was an astute move..."

I proposed "borrowing" the Longleat advert ("I have seen the Lions of Longleat") and the promoters went for it and had these stickers made.

Another popular move was the retention of Roger Jones as Team Manager.
John Payne applied to run the Shop. I remained as Trackside Photographer (voluntary, unpaid) until Mike Patrick moved to Oxfordshire and made Cowley his homebase stadium.

To make the stadium viable, Stock Car Racing returned, and an outdoor Sunday Market. For publicity, the market was opened by William Roache (Ken Barlow of Coronation Street) and, on another occasion, the Planet of the Apes team from Billy Smart's Circus (I think that is correct) attended.

William Roache

THE FIGHT TO SAVE THE STADIUM.

My press release in the Oxford Review, 15th October 1975.

SPEEDWAY ENDS BUT FANS SAY 'WE FIGHT ON!'

"We will fight on!" pledged the fans on Sunday. Recovering from the sudden shock of the sudden announcement of the closure of the Stadium at Cowley the Supporters' Club quickly started planning for next season.

If the team moves to Harringay the meetings will be held on Tuesdays in the season and a weekly coach could be run from Oxford to support the riders. There would be no change in the arrangements for the away matches, bookings being taken as often as possible.

In the meantime, petitions are being raised and action groups formed to retain the Stadium, and Dave Clinkard, chairman of The Supporters' Club, exhorted the spectators to write to their councillors and MPs to make them aware of the great following this family sport has.

One section of opinion voiced voiced strongly on Sunday was that speedway should continue at Cowley until a new sports stadium can be built in Oxford, housing several sports.

At the moment, facilities in Oxford fall far behind those in rural areas such as Bicester, Kidlington, and Witney. Although the Council may plead the cost, the speedway promoters offered £220,000 for Cowley and, if a combine was formed with other interests, this could be financially viable.

If no effort is made to save the stadium there will be a big gap in Oxford's social life when speedway, greyhounds and the nightly clubhouse have disappeared.

My press release in the Oxford Sports Scene, November 7th, 1975

PRESS COUNCIL FOR NEW STADIUM

In reply to the Secretary of State, a spokesman for the Department of the Environment has said that that matter has passed the stage where they are able to intervene.

His advice was "It is open to you, however, to press the Oxford City Council to provide alternative stadium facilities, to make a site available for a stadium, or to retain the present facilities until such time as alternative arrangements can be made".

The DOE came into the affair when the Stadium owners appealed against refusal of planning permission for houses on the site of the stadium. An inquiry was held in September 1974 and all following quotations are from the official report to the Secretary of State.

The report extends to 12 pages and is descriptive of the area involved, local facilities, etc. However, a recurring theme in the report makes its first appearance in paragraph 8:

"A proposed replacement site for the stadium lies about 2 miles to the west on the city side of the southern ring road at it's junction with Abingdon Road (4144). It consists of an expanse of rough grass falling gently to a stream with the main channel of the River Thames further east".

It is now known that no new stadium is planned for the Oxford area but at the time of the inquiry it does seem that the possibility of resiting the stadium may have influenced the final decision in favour of the appeal.

The following paragraphs are self-explanatory:

"Oxford is large enough to support a sports complex, possibly incorporating the local football club, and the appellants would be interested in such a project. Meanwhile, the present stadium could doubtless continue profitably with substantial capital expenditure.

"The alternative is to transfer the stadium to a more suitable location. A site has recently been found at the junction of Abingdon Road and the ring road, the latter providing proper vehicular approach. It is well away from dwellings and has the attraction of a frontage to the River Thames which could become a feature of the development.

"The site would not be available until a new stadium is constructed: i.e. for at least two years and a further two years would elapse before any of the houses were occupied..... Concern for the loss of entertainment facilities at the stadium would be overcome by the proposals to transfer the stadium to a new site....

" While the appellants allege that the present stadium is becoming uneconomic they have not proved that the site could not be satisfactorily redeveloped with additional or alternative sporting facilities to meet the needs of the city."

The Inspector concluded: "I recognise the desirability of securing the re-instatement of the stadium on a new site so that its leisure facilities for the community can be continued."

These previously unpublished reports of the appeal throw new light on puzzling facts surrounding the closure of the stadium.

What I recall about the Abingdon Road/ring road site is that it was prone to flooding most winters, being part of the Thames flood plain.

Reading this now, for supporters at other stadiums, it must resonate with the loss of stadiums for quick profits of housing development.

LETTERS TO THE PAPERS:

"Why do Oxford City Council try to give the impression to the public that if Cowley Stadium was purchased for housing there would be no costs to the ratepayers?
They have stated the size of the commitment if the stadium were leased to a co-operative of supporters: in the region of £44000, which are the debt fees for the loan required. The debt
fees for building would be £30000 per annum and the Government will only give a grant towards a smaller part of this.
Therefore, over three years the ratepayers will be subsidising the pockets of Bristol Stadiums. And can the Council guarantee that the houses will be built immediately after this time?
If the co-operative formed from members of SOS, city council, and residents of Blackbird Leys can offer a rent and profit participation to the Council, which can go a long way to covering the debt charges on the fixtures (five years) and what it will cost anyway, then it must be their duty to ensure that the stadium remains for the permanent use of the residents of Oxford."

Keith Lawson

While I don't have Mr Montague's letter, it is pretty obvious he had a whinge and a putdown about losing British League for National League.

THE NEW SPIRIT OF OXFORD STADIUM

"Mr Montague's letter (Sporting Postbag, Feb 27) regarding proposed speedway plans, is most disappointing. Has he not kept abreast of the battle to retain the sport in the city?
Every Oxford supporter is desperately sad to see the attractive Rebels team transfer to White City.

Promoters Dugard and Dunton, informed of the closedown last October, explored every avenue to keep the team at Cowley. Finally, when all seemed hopeless, they decided to make the move to London.

However, the magnificent SOS Committee in their unstinting efforts finally persuaded Oxford City Council to lease them the complex for a minimum of two years.

Already a new spirit is born. Thanks to the hard working enthusiasts and committee, the stadium is taking on a new appearance.

At least we are still assured of our Thursday evening entertainment, many new, exciting riders and visiting teams, unpredictable racing, and a host of junior talent to call on from the training school.

Fortunately, Roger Jones has agreed to return to the speedway business; he and the promoters are determined to make the new venture a success.

Local support is essential if premier speedway is ever to return to Oxford in the future. Meanwhile, we can still support the Rebels on their visits to Reading and Swindon.

Hopefully, all loyal fans will support this project and, if possible, help with the weekend 'work-ins' to improve the stadium.

Criticism would be better reserved at this stage, only time will prove if all the hard work and enthusiasm shown throughout the winter was worthwhile."

I. J. Belcher, Abingdon

GIVE NEW LEAGUE A CHANCE

"With reference to G.H. Montague's letter, I suspect that the majority of Oxford Speedway supporters are, like me, waiting until they have sampled Second Division racing at Cowley.
Let's hope that all supporters, past and present, will give this venture a chance to succeed, for surely Second Division is better than none at all and it at least leaves open a possibility (however remote) of a return to the First Division some time in the future if it can be shown that Oxford deserves it. As far as reverting to the title of the Cheetahs, as Shakespeare (William not Malcolm) said, 'What's in a name?'"

L.C. Green, Oxford

WE WILL HAVE QUALITY

"I am glad to say that I know many Oxford Rebel supporters that disagree with Mr Montague. Rather, I should say, 'speedway supporters', for over the last three weekends I have worked with volunteers at Cowley Stadium preparing it for its reopening and among them are supporters from 1949 to the present day, young and old.

Upset as we are at losing the best ever team at Oxford, we realise that the stadium must be saved first, because you cannot run speedway on a building site.

Harry Bastable, the new promoter, came to the stadium last week and said to the Committee that if we are successful in arranging a longer reprieve it is his intention to bring First Division racing back.

Meanwhile, people like Lynn Doolan, the top supporter at Oxford, and myself (Official Photographer for the Rebels for the last two seasons) are looking forward to seeing speedway back after witnessing what seemed like the death blow last year.

If Mr Montague is worried about the quality of the racing I can only presume he has never seen a New National League match and is basing his comments from witnessing these young lads in second half events against premier riders.

He can look forward to an exciting season watching the up-and-comers match races with BL riders, four team tournaments and inter-divisional cup matches.
Before anyone knocks NNL please come and watch first."

Keith Lawson, SOS Committee.

THE BIG CLEAN (pre-season)

Paint courtesy of Manders; effort courtesy of numerous fans.

A great feeling as people turned up to clean and paint and dig. Shale from outside the speedway track was recovered back inside. Lampposts and fencing painted. Bernard Crapper had a roller and whitewashed walls and I nearly wet myself when I saw him – the abominable snowman, covered by back spray, even to covering his spectacles so that when he took them off he had clear rings around his eyes. No photo, I am sad to say.

Radio Oxford with Mick "Foreman" Harris.

Fans painting the fencing

Reclaiming the shale from beyond the racetrack.

The digger cost nothing – the son of Derek Joyce brought it along.

Nothing got missed, not even the tops of the lamps!

PETE JARMAN'S SPEEDWAY SCHOOL

In the closed season, "Speedy" Pete Jarman ran a speedway school at the stadium. Among his alumni, Pip Lamb.

Pip Lamb gets personal advice
Pip's dad (in hat and holding flag) looks on

PETE JARMAN'S SPEEDWAY SCHOOL

Memories of what the stadium looked like in the '70s.

Colin Gooddy

The conditions were filthy on this day. One trainee had an accident and an ambulance had to be called. Pip's dad asked if anyone had a pen and, thinking he meant to take details down for the Accident Book, I handed over my favourite Parker ballpoint. "Here, lad, bite on this" and the pen was ruined. Tool of the trade for a journalist but not tax deductible.

16

PRESS DAY March 1976

The day coincided with the Press Day at White City so the speedway press did not attend, but we had local media as well as myself. Not all the riders were available to attend. I am not sure we had even signed everyone by then.

Mal Corradine, Harry Bastable, Harry MacLean

Mick Handley and Dave Clinkard

Harry Bastable's daughter?

Lord and Lady Mayor (Bill and Mrs Fagg) of Oxford

Mal Corradine

Roger Jones said "*Malcolm Corradine is on the comeback trail and has rekindled all his old fire and interest that he showed at Birmingham a couple of years ago.*"

Brian Leonard

Roger Jones would say "*Brian is taking this opportunity to try and regain his previous useful form and could prove an asset if he makes the team.*"

Harry MacLean

Harry Bastable

Harry MacLean

Mick Handley

Roger Jones' opinion "*In Mick Handley we have a rider with a great deal of British League experience and his record on this track is remembered by us all.*"

Roy Sizmore

Harry M, Mal and Mick with Harry B

PRESS DAY March 1976

This day was not exclusive for the speedway, it was an announcement that the stadium was under new management – a co-operative of fans of the various sports – and open for business.

Lord and Lady Mayor with the new Directors – Derek Joyce and Peter F. Jones (not the same Peter as on the SOS).

With the stock people

The financial backers of the stadium – Derek Joyce and Peter F. Jones
- they risked their money and we all benefited.

Derek Joyce and Peter F. Jones had known each other for around 20 years, their paths having crossed in the construction and building industry. It was as lovers of Greyhound Racing that they put up the finances to keep the stadium open, albeit there were only 2 years on the table in which to prove the viability.

Four of the SOS Committee became (unpaid) Directors of the Stadium to assist them – myself, M. Massey, A. Baker, Peter Jones.

PRESS DAY March 1976

The editor of the free paper, the Oxford Journal, attended and wrote a big piece on the event. Unfortunately, he mixed old news with new. It had been true that the Committee had talked about standing for election as councillors, but that had been a tactic to shake up the complacency of the council (and it seemed to have worked). However, the editor put it into his report as current news, which drew attention from the good news.
Don't let facts get in the way of a good headline!

It was a day where the rift with the old owners, Bristol Stadium, and the new seemed to have healed over. Clark Osborne, former General Manager, said, " I never expected to be handing over the stadium in such good an atmosphere. The swift negotiations that took place when two businessmen joined the co-operative quickly enabled the leasing of the equipment."

[*The message to today's fans fighting for the stadium is "find the money men (or women)" because spirit and campaigning is not enough.*]

The Lord Mayor – Councillor Bill Fagg – said how right the SOS were in pressing for the stadium to be kept open. "If the people of Oxford supported the stadium and proved it a success, then it would make the case for retention much stronger in two years time."

That two year reprieve was the motivation that had brought the fans in to renovate the stadium and for me to give so much time and effort throughout 1976 to try to make it a success. For my love of speedway I worked ceaselessly to promote our sport and the other activities at Cowley, not seeking praise (luckily, as it never came) or pay but determined that the although the battle had been won, we still had a war to win.

I did PR work for the stadium, photos for the various activities, helped organise events, looked out acts for live entertainment in the bar, did doorwork, took the racing finish photos of greyhounds - all voluntary work because the job of securing the stadium was not done with the new lease.

OXFORD CHEETAHS v EASTBOURNE

18 March 1976

38-40

(Challenge)

Team Manager: Roger Jones   Team Manager (Eagles): Arthur Nutley

RIDERS INDIVIDUAL SCORE CHART													
OXFORD	1	2	3	4	5	T	EASTBOURNE	1	2	3	4	5	T
1 Mick Handley	1	2*	2	1		6	1 Steve Weatherley	3	2	3	3		11
2 Mal Corradine	0	3	0	1*		4	2 Eric Dugard	2*	1*	3	2*		8
3 Steve Holden	1	0	N	N		1	3 Roger Abel	0	0				0
4 Carl Askew	3	3	3	3		12	4 Colin Richardson	2	1	0	1		4
5 Roy Sizmore	1	0	2*	2		5	5 ~~Mike Sampson~~						
6 Harry MacLean	2	3	2	0	0	7	6 Steve Naylor	0	1	1	2		4
7 Kevin Young	1*	1	1			3	7 Ian Fletcher	3	2*	2	0	0	7
							8 Pete Jarman	F	3	3			6
						38							40

Ht 01: Weatherley, Dugard, Handley, Corradine   72.0   1 - 5

Ht 02: Fletcher, MacLean, Young, Naylor   73.6   4 - 8

Ht 03: Askew, Richardson, Sizmore, Jarman (f exc)   72.6   8 -10

Ht 04: MacLean, Fletcher, Holden, Abel   72.5   12 -12

Ht 05: Askew, Weatherley, Dugard, Sizmore   70.8   15 -15

Ht 06: Corradine, Handley, Naylor, Abel   73.2   20 -16

Ht 07: Jarman, MacLean, Richardson, Holden   71.5   22 -20

Ht 08: Dugard, Fletcher, Young, Corradine   72.0   23 -25

Ht 09: Askew, Sizmore, Naylor, Fletcher   70.6   28 -26

Ht 10: Jarman, Handley, Corradine, Richardson   72.0   31 -29

Ht 11: Weatherley, Dugard, Young, MacLean   71.0   32 -34

Ht 12: Askew, Naylor, Handley, Abel   72.0   36 -36

Ht 13: Weatherley, Sizmore, Richardson, MacLean   70.2   38 -40

OXFORD CHEETAHS v EASTBOURNE   18 March 1976   38-40

Little wonder the visitors won – as Oxford's "supply" team, their riders had greater experience around Cowley and riding with a team mate than the newly formed Cheetahs. Best result of the night was the late arriving (his name wasn't even in the programme and had to be pencilled in) Carl Askew, who scored an immaculate 12 point maximum.

Steve "Eccles" Holden struggled in this meeting and Carl Askew recalls that Eccles did not have a rocker cover for his engine and rode with a helmet cover over it. I became good mates with Steve that year and he later told me that, as a lure to get him to leave Stoke (where he was doing well), the promoters had promised him a bike, which never happened. It would be a poor season for Steve and he eventually gave up his promising career in speedway. We had some fun that year and I was sorry when he did not return in 1977. We had only just remade contact, via Facebook, when he was taken from us. I never did beat him at pool.

Phil Bass did not make it in time and Roy Sizmore rode in his place, scoring a credible 5 points (plus 1 bonus).

We had a big parade of the SOS Committee as well as the riders.

My restoration work on the wall stands out – quite a lot of hairy moments up a wooden ladder balanced on the flatbed of a truck to bring the name and cheetahs back to life. I do not like heights.

Immediately a favourite with the fans – Carl Askew

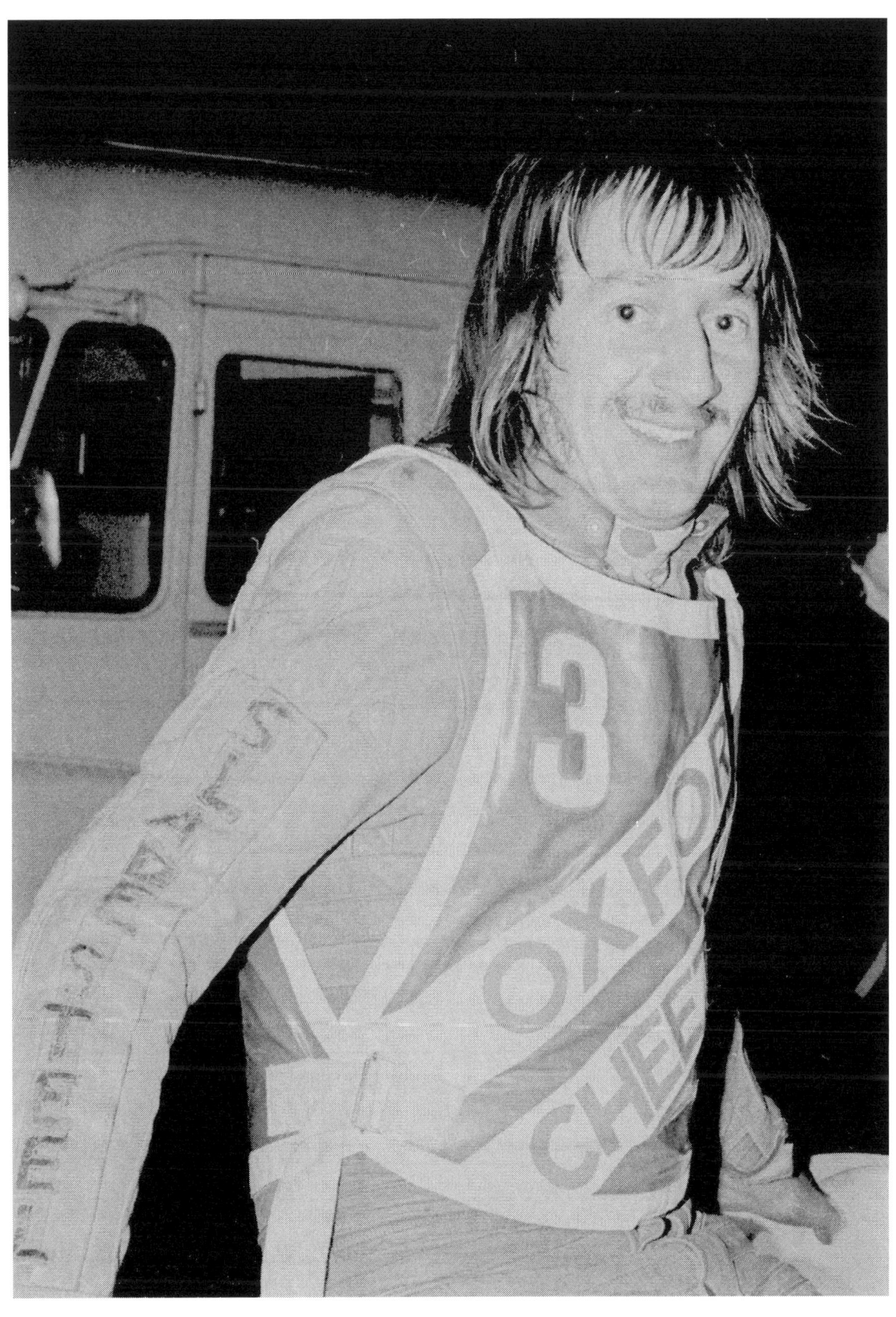

Steve "Eccles" Holden.

Kevin Young

No stranger to the Oxford track – Colin Richardson

My family used to run speedway here - Eric Dugard

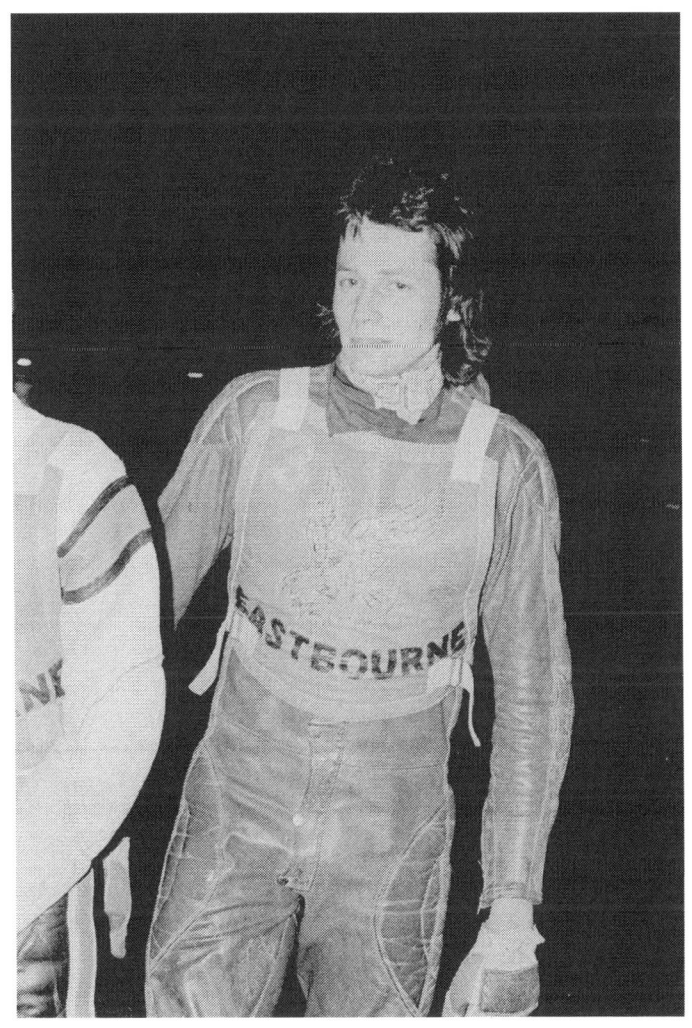

Roger Abel

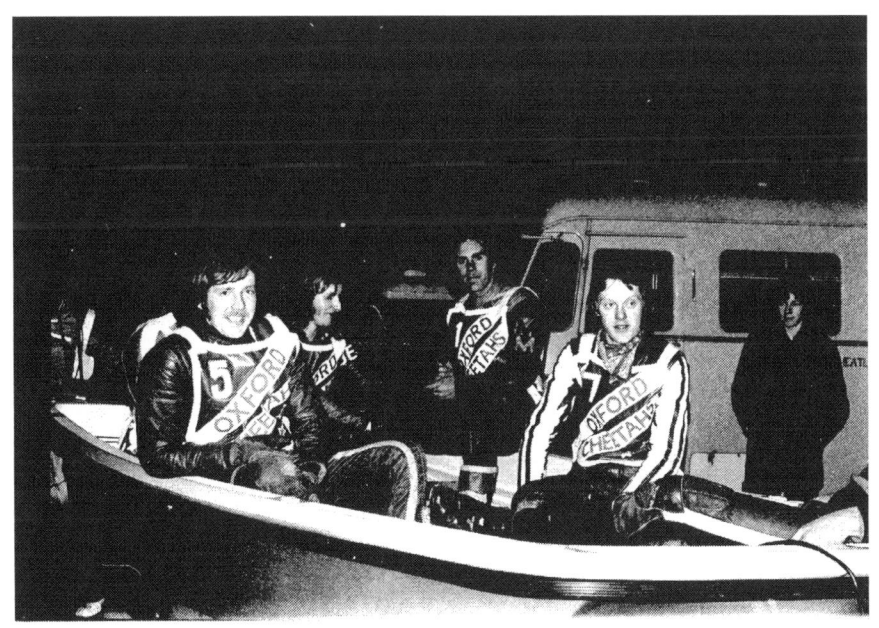

Roy Sizmore, Mal Corradine, Mick Handley, and Kevin Young

OXFORD CHEETAHS v VETLANDA

25th March 1976

57-21

(International Challenge Match)

Team Manager: Roger Jones   Team Manager (Vetlanda):

RIDERS INDIVIDUAL SCORE CHART													
OXFORD	1	2	3	4	5	T	VETLANDA	1	2	3	4	5	T
1 Mick Handley	1	3	3	3		10	1 Bo Wirebrand	2	2	1	2		7
2 Mal Corradine	3	2*	2*	2*		9	2 Willy Karlsson	0	0	1	0		1
3 Brian Leonard	2*	1*	2*	3		8	3 Karl-Erik Claesson	1	0	2	0		3
4 Phil Bass	3	1	1	1		6	4 Stefan Johansson	0	0	0	1*		1
5 Carl Askew	2*	3	3	X		8	5 Lars-Ake Andersson	1	3	1	2		7
6 Harry MacLean	2*	3	2			7	6 Borje Klingberg	1	1	0			2
7 Kevin Young	3	3	3			9	7 Goran Waltersson	0	0	0			0
						57							21

Vetlanda (Swedish Champions) would have a very disappointing UK tour – nearly every team they raced against scored over 50 points.

Ht 01: Corradine, Wirebrand, Handley, Karlsson	71.2	4 - 2	
Ht 02: Young, MacLean, Klingberg, Waltersson	71.8	9 - 3	
Ht 03: Bass, Askew, Andersson, Johansson	72.5	14 - 4	
Ht 04: MacLean, Leonard, Claesson, Waltersson	69.8	19 - 5	
Ht 05: Askew, Wirebrand, Bass, Karlsson	71.5	23 - 7	
Ht 06: Handley, Corradine, Klingberg, Claesson	69.6	28 - 8	
Ht 07: Andersson, MacLean, Leonard, Johansson	70.8	31 -11	
Ht 08: Young, Corradine, Karlsson, Waltersson	70.8	36 -12	
Ht 09: Askew, Claesson, Bass, Klingberg	70.0	40 -14	
Ht 10: Handley, Corradine, Andersson, Johansson	71.0	45 -15	
Ht 11: Young, Leonard, Wirebrand, Karlsson	70.1	50 -16	
Ht 12: Handley, Andersson, Bass, Claesson	70.2	54 -18	
Ht 13: Leonard, Wirebrand, Johansson, Askew (exc)	71.2	57 -21	

Carl Askew would set the NL Track Record in the second half at 68.8 secs.

NB the lighting failed on the pits bend stands and the fans were in darkness.

OXFORD CHEETAHS v VETLANDA

Mick Handley: "*I warned you last week that I could see us beginning to click and, against the Swedish lads, we really put it together. Honestly, I never enjoyed my speedway as much as I am here at Cowley.*

It's the same with the rest of the team; when you hear your name being shouted by the supporters it gives you a tremendous sensation. It makes you feel 10 feet tall.

I am desperately trying to save money at the moment, in the hope that, in the not too distant future, I will be able to afford a four-valve conversion for my Jawa. They appear to be much faster out of the gate and, who knows, Cuddly's [Carl Askew] track record may be brought down even further."

No well-paid riders unless at the very top – most had other jobs to survive financially. I believe Mick was a bricklayer at this time. In 1975, Mal Corradine had taken a break from racing in England as he could earn more on the continent – something that sounds familiar today.

The financial support from the fans was crucial if a team was to ride and the Supporters' Club took the profits from the stadium shop and coach trips to boost the riders' position.

Steve Holden had been given lodging with George Squires and Dave Clinkard until Clink organised a caravan in the pits. Steve was also welcome at my home for dinner so he could have a proper home-cooked meal. Steve earned a bit by DJing at the stadium club after meetings and on Sundays. He and Cliff Anderson would also do track maintenance and put the boards up for speedway night, and I would pitch in sometimes when available.

Life would get harder for Steve when he didn't get the rides and when the disco worked dried up, plus losing track work to George Squires and Bill Spicer. Cliff did engine maintenance to earn.

Cliff Anderson (1978)

BOSTON BARRACUDAS v OXFORD CHEETAHS

28th March 1976

47-31

(Challenge Match)

Team Manager (Barracudas):   Team Manager: Roger Jones

RIDERS INDIVIDUAL SCORE CHART														
BOSTON	**1**	**2**	**3**	**4**	**5**	**T**	**OXFORD**	**1**	**2**	**3**	**4**	**5**	**6**	**T**
1 Billy Burton	3	3	3	3		12	1 Mick Handley	1	1	E	2			4
2 Andy Sims	2*	0	2*	0		4	2 Roy Sizmore	0	T	0	N			0
3 Rob Hollingworth	3	3	3	3		12	3 Brian Leonard	0	1*	3	2	1*		7
4 Steve Clarke	1*	0	0	0		1	4 Carl Askew	F	2	1	T	N		3
5 Stuart Cope	2	2	2	1		7	5 Phil Bass	3	3	0	1*	2		9
6 Paul Gilbert	2	2*	2*			6	6 Harry MacLean	0	T	1	1			2
7 Trevor Whiting	1*	3	1			5	7 Kevin Young	3	0	1	N	2	0	6
						47								**31**

A cold and windy Boston!

Ht 01: Burton, Sims, Handley, Sizmore	66.8	5 - 1
Ht 02: Young, Gilbert, Whiting, MacLean	68.6	8 - 4
Ht 03: Bass, Cope, Clarke, Young, Askew (f ns)	68.2	11 - 7
Ht 04: Hollingworth, Gilbert, Young, Leonard	66.4	16 - 8
Ht 05: Bass, Cope, Handley, Clarke	68.6	18 -12
Ht 06: Burton, Askew, Leonard, Sims	67.6	21 -15
Ht 07: Hollingworth, Gilbert, Askew, Bass	66.0	26 -16
Ht 08: Whiting, Sims, MacLean, Sizmore	68.8	31 -17
Ht 09: Leonard, Cope, MacLean, Clarke	68.4	33 -21
Ht 10: Burton, Leonard, Bass, Sims	67.6	36 -24
Ht 11: Hollingworth, Young, Whiting, Handley (ef)	67.0	40 -26
Ht 12: Burton, Bass, Leonard, Clarke	67.4	43 -29
Ht 13: Hollingworth, Handley, Cope, Young	66.8	47 -31

BOSTON BARRACUDAS v OXFORD CHEETAHS

BOSTON BARRACUDAS 1976

BOSTON BARRACUDAS v OXFORD CHEETAHS

Andy Sims

Rob Hollingworth

Billy Burton

Brian Leonard

BOSTON BARRACUDAS v OXFORD CHEETAHS

Heat 1: Carl Askew fell.

Part of the engine went through his boot and into his ankle. The medical team were surprised to find Carl had painted toenails! Something from the previous evening with female company.

Heat 2: Kevin Young

Heat 3: Phil Bass

Heat 4: Rob Hollingworth, Brian Leonard, Paul Gilbert and Kevin Young

Heat 5: Phil Bass

OXFORD CHEETAHS v PETERBOROUGH PANTHERS

1st April 1976

34-44

(Challenge Match)

Team Manager: Roger Jones   Team Manager (Panthers): Ron Orchard

RIDERS INDIVIDUAL SCORE CHART													
OXFORD	**1**	**2**	**3**	**4**	**5**	**T**	**PETERBOROUGH**	**1**	**2**	**3**	**4**	**5**	**T**
1 Mick Handley	1	1	2	2		6	1 Tony Featherstone	2*	0	3	2		7
2 Mal Corradine	0	0	T	T		0	2 Russ Osborne	3	3	3	2*		11
3 Brian Leonard	1*	2	1*	1	0	7	3 Brian Clark	3	3	3	3		12
4 Phil Bass	3	1*	1*	1*	1*	7	4 Ken Matthews	0	3	F	N		3
5 Carl Askew	2*	F	N	N		2	5 Alan Cowland	1	1	3	0		5
6 Harry MacLean	1*	2	2	0	3	8	6 Roy Carter	3	2*	0	0		5
7 Kevin Young	2	2	2	0		6	7 Ian Clark	0	0	N	1		1
						34							**44**

Ht 01: Osborne, Featherstone, Handley, Corradine   68.6   1 - 5

Ht 02: Carter, Young, MacLean, I.Clark   69.4   4 - 8

Ht 03: Bass, Askew, Cowland, Matthews   70.1   9 - 9

Ht 04: B.Clark, MacLean, Leonard, I.Clark   68.7   12 -12

Ht 05: Osborne, MacLean, Bass, Featherstone, Askew (f ns)   69.2   15 -15

Ht 06: B.Clark, Carter, Handley, Corradine   69.0   16 -20

Ht 07: Matthews, Leonard, Cowland, MacLean   69.5   18 -24

Ht 08: Osborne, Young, Bass, Carter   69.2   21 -27

Ht 09: B.Clark, Young, Bass, Carter (f rem)   69.2   24 -30

Ht 10: Cowland, Handley, Leonard, Matthews (f exc)   69.8   27 -33

Ht 11: Featherstone, Osborne, Leonard, Young   69.0   28 -38

Ht 12: B.Clark, Handley, Bass, Cowland   68.6   31 -41

Ht 13: MacLean, Featherstone, I.Clark, Leonard   69.6   34 -44

Once again the Cheetahs faced what, could be considered, track specialists – the other "supply" team for the Rebels in 1975.

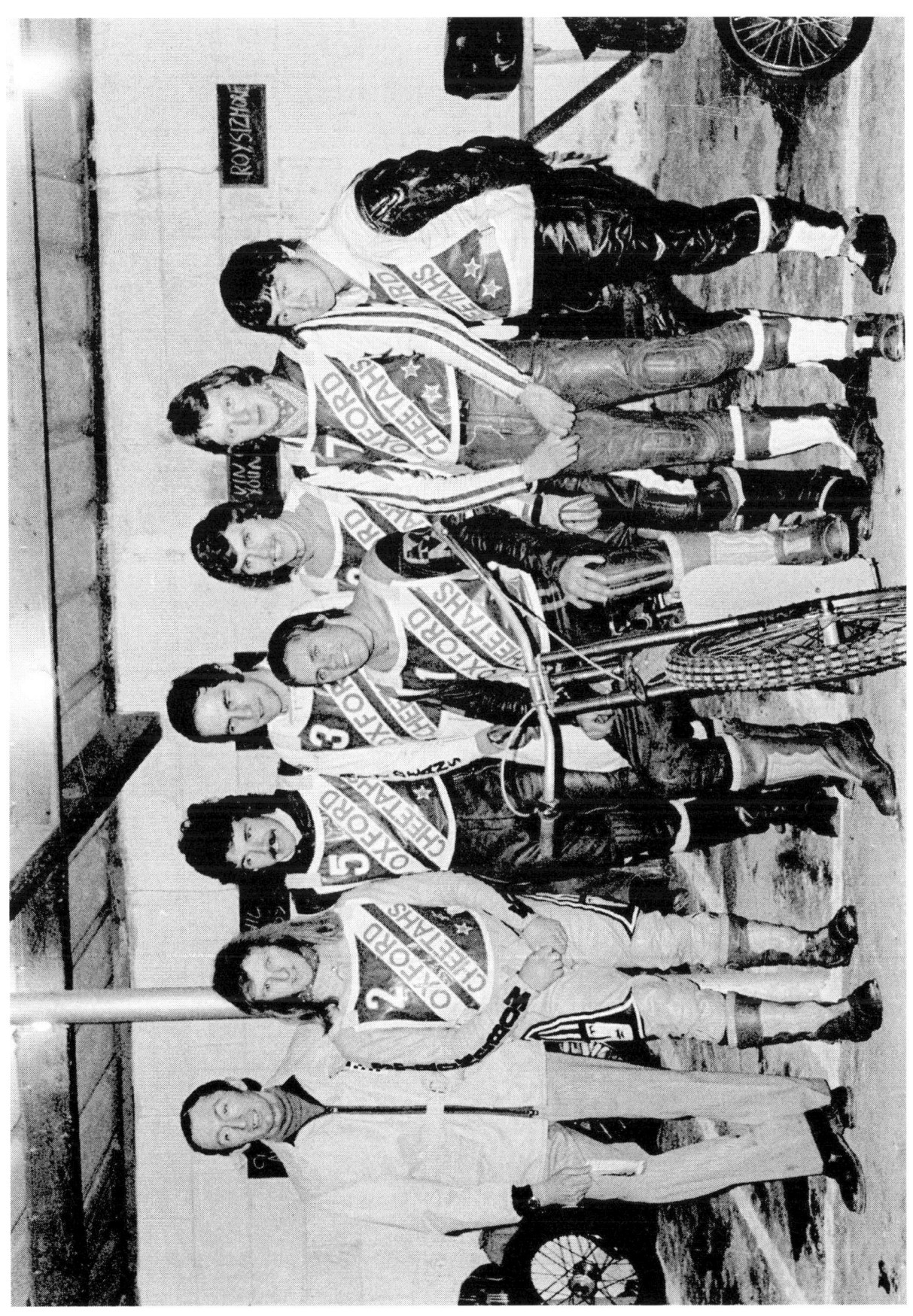

Brian Leonard

Mick Handley

Phil Bass

Tony Featherstone

When the flash isn't powerful enough to overcome the shortcomings of he stadium lighting (NB one of the reasons quoted by TV as to why they didn't cover speedway "The lighting is not good enough").

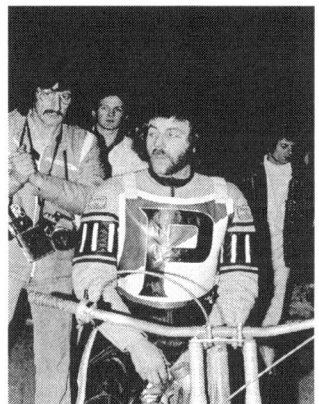

Photographer par excellence, Mike Patrick and Panther Russ Osborne

NEWCASTLE DIAMONDS v OXFORD CHEETAHS

5th April 1976

54-24

(National League)

Team Manager (Diamonds): Dave Younghusband*   Team Manager: Roger Jones

RIDERS INDIVIDUAL SCORE CHART													
NEWCASTLE	**1**	**2**	**3**	**4**	**5**	**T**	**OXFORD**	**1**	**2**	**3**	**4**	**5**	**T**
1 Tom Owen	3	2*	2*	3		10	1 Steve Holden	0	0	1	2		3
2 Ron Henderson	2*	3	3	3		11	2 Mal Corradine	1	T	N	0		1
3 Joe Owen	3	3	3	3		12	3 Brian Leonard	1	1	2	2		6
4 Andy Cusworth	3	1*	1	1		6	4 Carl Askew	2	3	2	1	1*	9
5 Brian Havelock	1	2	3	0		6	5 Phil Bass	0	0	0	0		0
6 Phil Michaelidies	X	2*	1			3	6 Harry MacLean	1	0	0	0		1
7 Tim Swales	2	2*	2*			6	7 Mick Handley	3	0	1			4
						54							**24**

* some programmes will say Ian Thomas – the possibility of a shared role?

Ht 01: T.Owen, Henderson, Corradine, Holden	69.6	5 - 1
Ht 02: Handley, Swales, MacLean, Michaelidies (exc tapes)	73.4	7 - 5
Ht 03: Cusworth, Askew, Havelock, Bass	71.0	11 - 7
Ht 04: J.Owen, Michaelidies, Leonard, Handley	70.4	16 - 8
Ht 05: Askew, Havelock, Cusworth, Holden	72.0	19 -11
Ht 06: Henderson, T.Owen, Leonard, MacLean	69.6	24 -12
Ht 07: J.Owen, Askew, Michaelidies, Bass	70.4	28 -14
Ht 08: Henderson, Swales, Handley, MacLean	70.2	33 -15
I lt 09: Havelock, Leonard, Cusworth, MacLean	71.0	37 -17
Ht 10: Henderson, T.Owen, Askew, Bass	70.2	42 -18
Ht 11: J.Owen, Swales, Holden, Corradine	70.2	47 -19
Ht 12: T.Owen, Leonard, Cusworth, Bass	71.6	51 -21
Ht 13: J.Owen, Holden, Askew, Havelock	70.4	54 -24

JOE OWEN

TOM OWEN

STEVE HOLDEN

NEWCASTLE DIAMONDS v OXFORD CHEETAHS   5th April 1976

Steve Holden was booked to ride at Newcastle. Only there were a couple of problems – he didn't have a raceworthy bike and he did not have transport.

Our solution was to use the track spare and take the boot lid off my Ford Capri to fit it in. So that is what happened.

We drove up to Stoke on the Sunday and Steve directed us to a family, without advance notice, where I think he had lodged before. We were made very welcome and given dinner and the offer of beds for the night. At some point I realised that both Steve and my car keys were missing; he'd gone for a spin round the old haunts.

The next day we continued on to Newcastle. For a change from photography, and because it would get too dark to take racing photos, I stayed in the pits to look after the bike. He really needed a proper mechanic as we could not get the silencer to stay on and it came adrift, causing him to retire in two races. I upset Brian Leonard by using his oil for Steve, then made it up to him by fuelling and oiling his bike as well.

After the meeting we were invited to a party and Mick Handley came with us while someone else drove his gear home. Wasn't much of a party and we tried sleeping on the floor but eventually decided to hit the road. Mick took over some of the driving as I was falling asleep at the wheel. What I remember most is being flashed by oncoming cars to dip my headlamps, but they were dipped – the weight of the bike in the boot was tilting the car. Anyway, we dropped Mick off in Doncaster and pulled over to catch some sleep in the car.

Later, we would arrive at Leicester to watch the England Lions v the England World Cup Team....

ENGLAND LIONS v ENGLAND WORLD TEAM CUP

6th April 1976

42-36

(at Leicester)

Team Manager: John Berry   Team Manager: Len Silver

RIDERS INDIVIDUAL SCORE CHART													
ENGLAND LIONS	**1**	**2**	**3**	**4**	**5**	**T**	**ENGLAND WTC**	**1**	**2**	**3**	**4**	**5**	**T**
1 Chris Pusey	1	1	0	3		5	1 Ray Wilson	F	N	N	T		0
2 John Davis	3	F	0	N		3	2 John Louis	2	1	2	1		6
3 Peter Collins	3	3	3	3		12	3 Martin Ashby	1*	3	1	2	1*	8
4 Doug Wyer	0	2*	3	0		5	4 Dave Jessup	2*	2	3	2		9
5 Chris Morton	1	3	2*	0		6	5 Malcolm Simmons	3	2*	1*	2*	1*	9
6 Dave Morton	3	F	0			3	6 Terry Betts	1	0	T	0		1
7 Gordon Kennett	2*	3	1	2*		8	7 Reg Wilson	0	2	1*	0		3
						42							**36**

Ht 01: Davis, Louis, Pusey, Ray Wilson (f exc)   66.4   4 -2

Ht 02: D.Morton, Kennett, Betts, Reg Wilson   65.6   9 - 3

Ht 03: Simmons, Jessup, C.Morton, Wyer   65.8   10 - 8

Ht 04: Collins, Reg Wilson, Ashby, D.Morton (f exc)   66.4   13 -11

Ht 05: C.Morton, Wyer, Louis, Betts   66.6   18 -12

Ht 06: Ashby, Simmons, Pusey, Davis (f exc)   67.0   19 -17

Ht 07: Collins, Jessup, Simmons, D.Morton   65.0   22 -20

Ht 08: Kennett, Louis, Reg Wilson, Davis   65.4   25 -23

Ht 09: Wyer, C.Morton, Ashby, Betts   67.2   30 -24

Ht 10: Jessup, Simmons, Kennett, Pusey   65.4   31 -29

Ht 11: Collins, Kennett, Louis, Reg Wilson   67.4   36 -30

Ht 12: Pusey, Ashby, Simmons, Wyer   66.6   39 -33

Ht 13: Collins, Jessup, Ashby, C.Morton   65.4   42 -36

Peter Collins 2017

ENGLAND LIONS v ENGLAND WORLD TEAM CUP 6th April 1976

I liked Blackbird Road as a stadium and I was particularly fond of the pasties they sold.

We drove straight in – I think the guy on the gate thought we were riding, as we came with a bike.

Huge excitement was the arrival of Freddie Starr, who, at this time was one of the biggest names in showbiz. He wasn't booked for entertainment, I believe he turned up with Reg Wilson, but he played up to the crowd. I was taking a team photo, dipped into the "photographer's squat" so as not to take a photo looking down on the riders. As I was focusing, I wondered why the team was so amused... then Freddie goosed me.

It was a good meeting. A bit of a shock that Ray Wilson, whose home track this was, should have such a bad meet. Peter Collins would be unbeaten – this is the year he would become World Champion.

CHRIS MORTON

CHRIS PUSEY

DOUG WYER

GORDON KENNETT

JOHN DAVIS

MARTIN ASHBY

PETER COLLINS

TERRY BETTS

"Why aren't they looking this way? I need to take a photo."

Then Freddie Starr goosed me!

Taking the plaudits for assaulting me.

John Berry and Dave Morton

OXFORD CHEETAHS v BOSTON BARRACUDAS

8th April 1976

42-36

(National League)

Team Manager: Roger Jones   Team Manager (Barracudas):

RIDERS INDIVIDUAL SCORE CHART													
OXFORD	**1**	**2**	**3**	**4**	**5**	**T**	**BOSTON**	**1**	**2**	**3**	**4**	**5**	**T**
1 Mick Handley	1	N	2	2		5	1 Billy Burton	2	0	0	1		3
2 Mal Corradine	3	2	3	0		8	2 Trevor Whiting	0	N	1*	3		4
3 Brian Leonard	0	1	N	N		1	3 Rob Hollingworth	3	3	3	2	3	14
4 Phil Bass	2*	3	1	1*		7	4 Andy Sims	0	T	1	F		1
5 Carl Askew	3	2*	3	3		11	5 Stuart Cope	1	2*	3	F		6
6 Harry MacLean	0	2	0	2	2*	6	6 Steve Clarke	1	0	N			1
7 Kevin Young	2	1*	0	1*		4	7 Paul Gilbert	3	1	1	2	0	7
						42							**36**

Ht 01: Corradine, Burton, Handley, Whiting	68.4	4 - 2
Ht 02: Gilbert, Young, Clarke, MacLean	68.5	6 - 6
Ht 03: Askew, Bass, Cope, Sims	69.5	11 - 7
Ht 04: Hollingworth, MacLean, Gilbert, Leonard	68.2	13 -11
Ht 05: Bass, Askew, Gilbert, Burton	69.5	18 -12
Ht 06: Hollingworth, Corradine, Young, Clarke	68.0	21 -15
Ht 07: Hollingworth, Cope, Leonard, MacLean	67.8	22 -20
Ht 08: Corradine, Gilbert, Whiting, Young	67.7	25 -23
Ht 09: Askew, Hollingworth, Bass, Gilbert	69.0	29 -25
Ht 10: Cope, Handley, Sims, Corradine	69.0	31 -29
Ht 11: Whiting, MacLean, Young, Burton	69.4	34 -32
Ht 12: Hollingworth, Handley, Bass, Cope (f)	68.2	37 -35
Ht 13: Askew, MacLean, Burton (f awarded), Sims (f)	68.2	42 -36

OXFORD CHEETAHS v BOSTON BARRACUDAS

Roger Jones:

"*Wasn't this a cracker? The Barracudas, who came to Cowley with every intention of showing the Cheetah's the way home, were turned away with no points.*

Main 'striking force", Carl Askew, flew around the Cowley track in a most impressive style (after his injury the week before) and in obtaining his paid maximum, was the only Cheetah to master the magnificent Boston #3, Rob Hollingworth.

Both Mal Corradine – who had a ding-dong battle with Hollingworth for the track record, and came out on top – and Phil Bass – who showed the great value of remounting the bike after a fall in heat 12 – was rewarded with third place, putting up sound supporting roles to Carl.

Both reserves, Harry MacLean and Kevin Young went well, providing some nail-biting entertainment. Our thanks must also go to the opposition though, for without them such an exciting match would not have been possible.

One final word must go to the supporters, who really spurred our boys on, particularly when the going got a bit hot towards heat 13. It felt really good to see them enjoying themselves at Cowley once more."

WORKINGTON COMETS v OXFORD CHEETAHS

9th April 1976

50-28

(National League)

Team Manager (Comets): Alan Middleton   Team Manager: Roger Jones

RIDERS INDIVIDUAL SCORE CHART													
WORKINGTON	**1**	**2**	**3**	**4**	**5**	**T**	**OXFORD**	**1**	**2**	**3**	**4**	**5**	**T**
1 Taffy Owen	3	3	3	3		12	1 Mick Handley	1	N	R	N		1
2 Roger Wright	2*	2*	2*	2*		8	2 Mal Corradine	0	1	1	1		3
3 Lou Sansom	3	3	3	3		12	3 Brian Leonard	2	0	3	2		7
4 Des Wilson	0	N	1	N		1	4 Carl Askew	1	1*	0	2		4
5 Colin Goad	2	2*	0	1		5	5 Phil Bass	3	1	2	1	1*	8
6 Chris Bevan	1	0	0	0		1	6 Harry MacLean	0	0	T	2*		2
7 Steve Lawson	3	3	3	2*		11	7 Kevin Young	2	1*	0	0		3
						50							**28**

Ht 01: Owen, Wright, Handley, Corradine   75.0   5 - 1

Ht 02: Lawson, Young, Bevan, MacLean   75.2   9 - 3

Ht 03: Bass, Goad, Askew, Wilson   75.4   11 - 7

Ht 04: Sansom, Leonard, Young, Bevan   74.4   14 -10

Ht 05: Lawson, Goad, Corradine, MacLean   75.0   19 -11

Ht 06: Owen, Wright, Bass, Leonard   75.4   24 -12

Ht 07: Sansom, Bass, Askew, Bevan   74.8   27 -15

Ht 08: Lawson, Wright, Corradine, Young   76.8   32 -16

Ht 09: Leonard, MacLean, Wilson, Goad   77.0   33 -21

Ht 10: Owen, Wright, Bass, Askew   75.4   38 -22

Ht 11: Sansom, Lawson, Corradine, Handley (ret)   75.0   43 -23

Ht 12: Owen, Leonard, Bass, Bevan   76.2   46 -26

Ht 13: Sansom, Askew, Goad, Young   75.0   50 -28

BERWICK BANDITS v OXFORD CHEETAHS

10 April 1976

46-32

(National League)

Team Manager (Bandits): Kenny Taylor   Team Manager: Roger Jones

RIDERS INDIVIDUAL SCORE CHART													
BERWICK	1	2	3	4	5	T	**OXFORD**	1	2	3	4	5	T
1 Mike Hiftle	2*	X	2*	1		5	1 Mick Handley	R	1	T	T		1
2 Willie Templeton	3	3	3	3		12	2 Mal Corradine	1	3	2	2	1	9
3 Graham Jones	3	3	3	2*		11	3 Brian Leonard	2	2	R	2		6
4 Eddie Argall	0	R	1	3		4	4 Phil Bass	1*	1*	1	0		3
5 Dave Gifford	3	2	3	3		11	5 Carl Askew	2	2	X	1*	0	5
6 Peter Waite	2	0	0			2	6 Harry MacLean	3	0	2			5
7 Frank Hall	R	1	0	F		1	7 Kevin Young	1	1*	1*			3
						46							**32**

Ht 01: Templeton, Hiftle, Corradine, Handley (ret)	76.0	5 - 1
Ht 02: MacLean, Waite, Young, Hall (ret)	79.6	7 - 5
Ht 03: Gifford, Askew, Bass, Argall	77.8	10 - 8
Ht 04: Jones, Leonard, Young, Waite	77.4	13 -11
Ht 05: Corradine, Gifford, Handley, Argall (ret)	78.2	15 -15
Ht 06: Templeton, Leonard, Hall, MacLean, Hiftle (exc)	77.4	19 -17
Ht 07: Jones, Askew, Bass, Waite	76.2	22 -20
Ht 08: Templeton, Corradine, Young, Hall	78.2	25 -23
Ht 09: Gifford, MacLean, Argall, Leonard (ret)	78.4	29 -25
Ht 10: Templeton, Hiftle, Bass, Askew (exc)	78.8	34 -26
Ht 11: Jones, Corradine, Askew, Hall (f)	78.0	37 -29
Ht 12: Argall, Leonard, Hiftle, Askew	78.4	41 -31
Ht 13: Gifford, Jones, Corradine, Bass	79.0	46 -32

One heck of a workload for the Cheetahs – racing on three consecutive nights – not allowing time to recovery or do proper maintenance on their machines.

OXFORD MAIL NEWS

13th April 1976

SUMMER POP AT THE STADIUM

Cowley Stadium's newly appointed Entertainments Manager, Mr Tony Dell, is planning a summer pop concert at the stadium with big name groups.

Mr Dell, a former Caroline and Luxembourg radio disc jockey, TV stunt man and actor, says he has deals in the pipeline for top artists at the stadium's club.

Mr Dell comes to the stadium after being Entertainments Manager for Butlins and host at a top night club.

Tony Dell (pictured here with Tony Blackburn) had been planning how to increase the entertainment value of Cowley Stadium. He organised the weekly discos (using Steve Holden and local Bob Beeches as DJs as well as taking turns himself). A Talent Show was run and the best musical acts got contracts to perform at Live Nights. The ambition was to run open air concerts in the arena.

Tony had been a DJ on Radio Caroline and Radio Luxembourg and had done TV work on popular soaps "Crossroads" and "Coronation Street".

TEESIDE TIGERS v OXFORD CHEETAHS

15th April 1976

43-34

(National League)

Team Manager (Tigers): Tony Coupland   Team Manager: Roger Jones

RIDERS INDIVIDUAL SCORE CHART													
TEESIDE	1	2	3	4	5	T	OXFORD	1	2	3	4	5	T
1 Tom Leadbitter	3	2*	3	3		11	1 Carl Askew	2	1	2*	0	2	7
2 Andy Cowan	1	3	0	N		4	2 Mal Corradine	F	3	3	2	1*	9
3 Pete Reading	3	3	3	3		12	3 Brian Leonard	2	1	1	2		6
4 Steve Wilcock	2*	0	2*	0		4	4 Phil Bass	X	2	2	1*		5
5 Alan Emerson	3	2	3	0		8	5 Steve Holden	N	0	1*	T		1
6 Pete Smith	0	F	1	0		1	6 Harry MacLean	3	F	N	N		3
7 Dave Levings	1	1	1			3	7 Kevin Young	2*	1*	0	T	0	3
						43							34

Ht 01: Leadbitter, Askew, Cowan, Corradine (f)	69.6	4 - 2
Ht 02: MacLean, Young, Levings, Smith	72.6	5 - 7
Ht 03: Emerson, Wilcock, Bass (exc), MacLean (f exc)	73.4	10 - 7
Ht 04: Reading, Leonard, Young, Smith (f)	70.2	13 -10
Ht 05: Corradine, Emerson, Askew, Wilcock	70.0	15 -14
Ht 06: Cowan, Leadbitter, Leonard, Young	70.2	20 -15
Ht 07: Reading, Bass, Smith, Holden	70.2	24 -17
Ht 08: Corradine, Askew, Levings, Cowan	71.2	25 -22
Ht 09: Emerson, Wilcock. Leonard, Young	71.4	30 -23
Ht 10: Leadbitter, Bass, Holden, Smith	69.8	33 -26
Ht 11: Reading, Corradine, Levings, Askew (f rem)	69.6	37 -28
Ht 12: Leadbitter, Leonard, Corradine, Wilcock	70.2	40 -31
Ht 13: Reading, Askew, Bass, Emerson	69.6	43 -34

OXFORD CHEETAHS v TEESIDE TIGERS

16th April 1976

43-35

(National League)

Team Manager: Roger Jones   Team Manager (Tigers): Tony Coupland

RIDERS INDIVIDUAL SCORE CHART													
OXFORD	**1**	**2**	**3**	**4**	**5**	**T**	**TEESIDE**	**1**	**2**	**3**	**4**	**5**	**T**
1 Carl Askew	3	2	3	3		11	1 Tom Leadbitter	2	1*	3	F		6
2 Mal Corradine	1	1*	2	F		4	2 Andy Cowan	0	2	3	1		6
3 Brian Leonard	2	2	2	3		9	3 Pete Reading	3	3	2	2	2	12
4 Phil Bass	1	3	1	1		6	4 Steve Wilcock	0	0	T	2		2
5 Steve Holden	3	0	N	N		3	5 Alan Emerson	2	3	1*	F		6
6 Roy Sizmore	1	0	1*			2	6 Pete Smith	2	0	0			2
7 Kevin Young	3	1*	3	0	1	8	7 Dave Levings	0	1	0			1
						43							**35**

Ht 01: Askew, Leadbitter, Corradine, Cowan	69.2	4 - 2
Ht 02: Young, Smith, Sizmore, Levings	68.5	8 - 4
Ht 03: Holden, Emerson, Bass, Wilcock (f rem)	70.6	12 - 6
Ht 04: Reading, Leonard, Levings, Sizmore	69.6	14 -10
Ht 05: Bass, Cowan, Leadbitter, Holden	69.0	17 -13
Ht 06: Reading, Askew, Corradine, Smith	68.2	20 -16
Ht 07: Emerson, Leonard, Sizmore, Wilcock	69.0	23 -19
Ht 08: Cowan, Corradine, Young, Levings	70.0	26 -22
Ht 09: Young, Reading, Bass, Smith	68.1	30 -24
Ht 10: Askew, Reading, Emerson, Corradine (f)	68.0	33 -27
Ht 11: Leadbitter, Leonard, Cowan, Young	70.4	35 -31
Ht 12: Askew, Reading, Bass, Emerson (f)	67.7	39 -33
Ht 13: Leonard, Wilcock, Young, Leadbitter (f)	69.0	43 -35

OXFORD CHEETAHS v TEESIDE TIGERS

Roger Jones' Report:

"Another exciting home match against the Tigers. Despite a very enthusiastic effort from the visitors' experienced side – especially Pete Reading – the Cheetahs came out on top.

Leading the scoring for the Cheetahs once more was Carl Askew,who rode extremely well, only dropping one point and equalling the track record.

Brian Leonard put up a very spirited performance, backing Askew's skill and determination with experience and hard graft.

Kevin Young also rode well, particularly when he beat Pete Reading in one of the fastest times of the day.

Steve "Eccles" Holden showed he is capable and worthy of a team place, despite being very bruised from the previous night's meeting.

Apart from being beaten away at Teeside, the Cheetahs suffered a severe blow when Harry MacLean, the brilliant young Scot, was involved in an accident, from which he received a broken wrist, broken forearm and broken shoulder.

Harry sends everyone at Cowley his best wishes and I am sure you all wish him a speedy recovery. Now that Harry is out of the team, we have increased our activities in respect of attaining another heat leader class rider to strengthen the Cheetahs in depth.

Once more we must apologise for the delay at the start of the meeting and also in the second half, caused by the starting gate sticking – this will be rectified."

NB Harry MacLean would not recover in time for this season and when, in 1977, he was available, the promoters did not want him.

OXFORD CHEETAHS v TEESIDE TIGERS

Phil Bass, Steve Holden, Roy Sizmore, Kevin Young

Carl Askew and Malcolm Corradine

OXFORD CHEETAHS v TEESIDE TIGERS

Brian Leonard

Phil Bass

Steve Holden

Roy Sizmore

OXFORD CHEETAHS v TEESIDE TIGERS

Kevin Young

Andy Cowan

Pete Reading

Steve Wilcock

OXFORD CHEETAHS v TEESIDE TIGERS

Carl Askew

OXFORD CHEETAHS v TEESIDE TIGERS

Heat 1: Mal Corradine, Carl Askew and Andy Cowan (yb)

Carl Askew

OXFORD CHEETAHS v TEESIDE TIGERS

Mal Corradine

Carl Askew

OXFORD CHEETAHS v TEESIDE TIGERS

Heat 2: Kevin Young.
Those ply boards had a secondary purpose – retain shale that otherwise would end up on the greyhound track, which had to be sheeted to protect it.

Heat 2: Pete Smith and Kevin Young

OXFORD CHEETAHS v TEESIDE TIGERS

Heat 3: Steve Holden, Steve Wilcock and Phil Bass

Heat 3: Alan Emerson and Phil Bass

OXFORD CHEETAHS v TEESIDE TIGERS

Heat 4: Pete Reading and Brian Leonard

Heat 4: Brian Leonard

OXFORD CHEETAHS v TEESIDE TIGERS

Heat 5: Steve Holden

OXFORD CHEETAHS v TEESIDE TIGERS

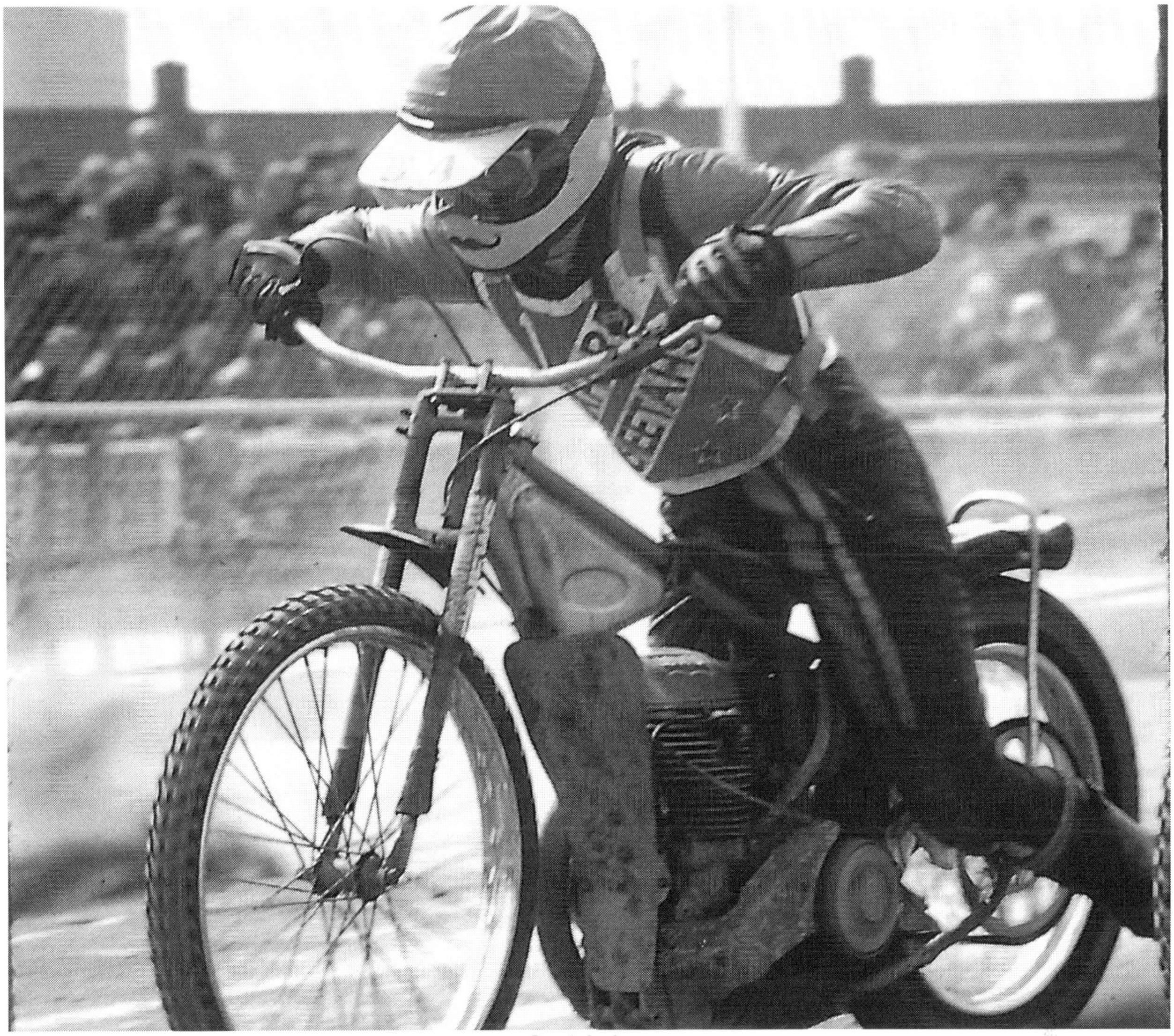

Carl Askew

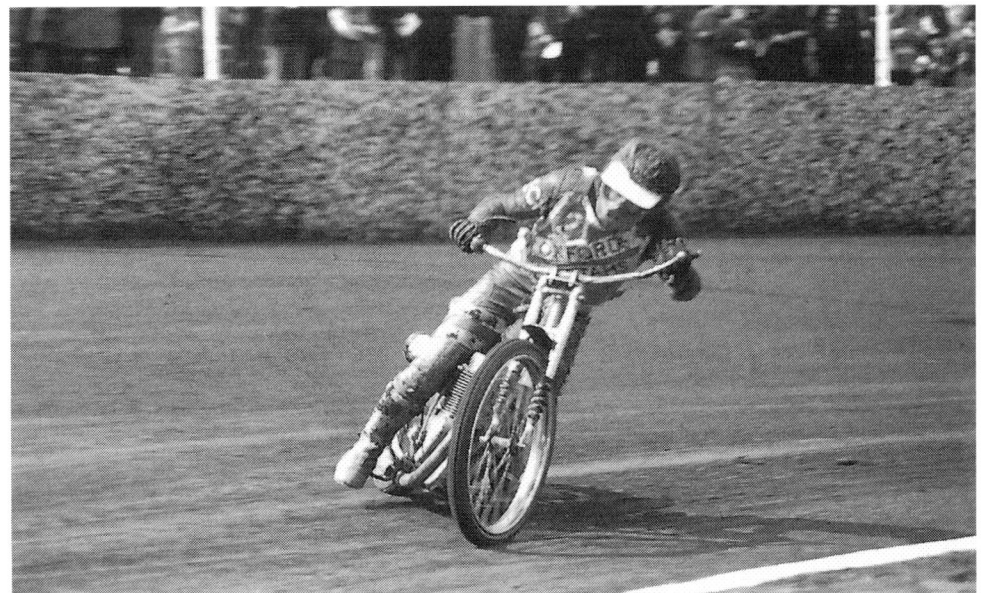

Mal Corradine

OXFORD CHEETAHS v TEESIDE TIGERS

Heat 7: Roy Sizmore, Steve Wilcock, Brian Leonard, Alan Emerson

Heat 8: Andy Cowan and Kevin Young

OXFORD CHEETAHS v TEESIDE TIGERS

Heat 9: Phil Bass and Pete Reading (Pete Smith fallen)

Heat 9: Kevin Young and Phil Bass, Pete Reading (w)

Heat 9: Kevin Young

Heat 9: Phil Bass

OXFORD CHEETAHS v TEESIDE TIGERS

Heat 10: Carl Askew and Alan Emerson

Heat 11: Brian Leonard and Tom Leadbitter

OXFORD CHEETAHS v TEESIDE TIGERS

"King of Cowley" 2nd Half event

sponsored by Hartford Motors

Steve Wilcock, Brian Leonard, Carl Askew and Mal Corradine

Presentation by Pete Cundy of Hartford Motors

OXFORD CHEETAHS v TEESIDE TIGERS

"King of Cowley" 2nd Half event

sponsored by Hartford Motors

The track staff, St John's people and Mike Patrick

Carl Askew, Steve Wilcock, Brian Leonard, Pete Cundy and Mal Corradine

EASTER PUBLICITY STUNT

As part of my unofficial, unpaid role of promoting the Cheetahs, I thought it would be a good idea if we took chocolate eggs to the Children's Ward of the John Radcliffe Hospital. As Steve Holden was on hand, living in a caravan at the stadium, he was the obvious choice to represent the team. I bought eggs with my own money but, thankfully, both the Supporters' Club and the Promoters, when they heard what I was doing, then wanted to be involved, so we were able to purchase more eggs.

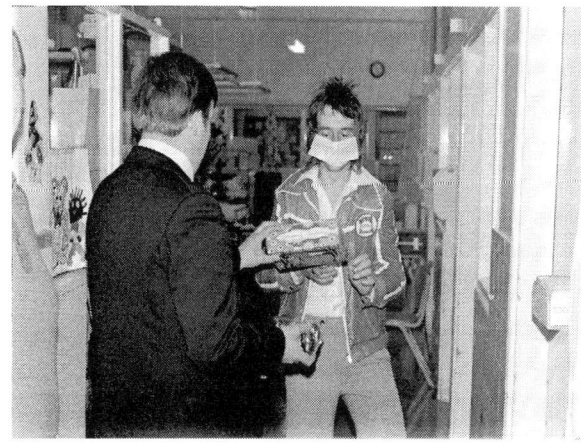 

In June, I would set up and manage a Stadium stall at the British Leyland Sports Day. Keith Pilcher attended to represent the Speedway, and the Stock Car people sent a car and driver. Les Windle (SOS Committee) lent his business transit van so we could transport bits and pieces, such as the garden tables I had retrieved from the neglected swimming pool of the White Buffalo and cleaned and painted.

Keith Pilcher

WEYMOUTH WIZARDS v OXFORD CHEETAHS

20th April 1976

40-38

(National League KOC Preliminary Round 1st Leg)

Team Manager (Wizards): Joe Bargery   Team Manager: Roger Jones

RIDERS INDIVIDUAL SCORE CHART													
WEYMOUTH	1	2	3	4	5	T	**OXFORD**	1	2	3	4	5	T
1 Chris Robins	3	3	3	3		12	1 Carl Askew	1*	2*	1*	2		6
2 Geoff Swindells	0	0	N	N		0	2 Mal Corradine	2	3	3	2		10
3 Martin Yeates	3	3	3	3		12	3 Brian Leonard	1	2	3	2		8
4 Roger Stratton	2*	0	1*	0		3	4 Phil Bass	1	1*	0	N		2
5 Vic Harding	3	1	2	1		7	5 Mick Handley	F	2	2	1		5
6 Garry May	0	2*	N	1	1	4	6 Kevin Young	1	1*	0			2
7 Trevor Charley	2	0	0	0		2	7 Roy Sizmore	3	R	2*	0		5
						40							**38**

Ht 01: Robins, Corradine, Askew, Swindells   70.9   3 - 3

Ht 02: Sizmore, Charley, Young, May   72.5   5 - 7

Ht 03: Harding, Stratton, Bass, Handley (f exc)   72.1   10 - 8

Ht 04: Yeates, May, Leonard, Sizmore (ret)   73.3   15 - 9

Ht 05: Corradine, Askew, Harding, Stratton   72.0   16 -14

Ht 06: Robins, Leonard, Young, Swindells   72.7   19 -17

Ht 07: Yeates, Handley, Bass, Charley   73.0   22 -20

Ht 08: Corradine, Sizmore, May, Charley   72.8   23 -25

Ht 09: Leonard, Harding, Stratton, Young   74.4   26 -28

Ht 10: Robins, Handley, May, Bass   73.5   30 -30

Ht 11: Yeates, Corradine, Askew, Charley   72.6   33 -33

Ht 12: Robins, Leonard, Handley, Stratton   74.0   36 -36

Ht 13: Yeates, Askew, Harding, Sizmore   73.6   40 -38

OXFORD CHEETAHS v WEYMOUTH WIZARDS

22nd April 1976

48-30

(National League KOC Preliminary Round 2nd Leg)

Team Manager: Roger Jones   Team Manager (Wizards): Joe Bargery

RIDERS INDIVIDUAL SCORE CHART													
OXFORD	1	2	3	4	5	T	WEYMOUTH	1	2	3	4	5	T
1 Carl Askew	2	2*	1	3		8	1 Martin Yeates	3	2	2	3	3	13
2 Mick Handley	1*	3	3	3		10	2 Gerald Purkiss	0	0	1*	1		2
3 Brian Leonard	2	0	0	1*		3	3 Chris Robins	3	1	1	0		5
4 Phil Bass	2*	1	2*	1		6	4 Roger Stratton	0	1	0	0		1
5 Mal Corradine	3	3	3	2		11	5 Vic Harding	1	3	2	2		8
6 Roy Sizmore	2*	1*	2			5	6 Garry May	0	0	0			0
7 Kevin Young	3	0	2			5	7 Trevor Charley	1	0	T			1
						48							30

Agg: Oxford 86 - 70 Weymouth

Ht 01: Yeates, Askew, Handley, Purkiss	68.0	3 - 3
Ht 02: Young, Sizmore, Charley, May	70.0	8 - 4
Ht 03: Corradine, Bass, Harding, Stratton	69.4	13 - 5
Ht 04: Robins, Leonard, Sizmore, Charley	68.7	16 - 8
Ht 05: Corradine, Yeates, Bass, Purkiss	68.0	20 -10
Ht 06: Handley, Askew, Robins, May	69.4	25 -11
Ht 07: Harding, Sizmore, Stratton, Leonard	69.0	27 -15
Ht 08: Handley, Yeates, Purkiss, Young	69.0	30 -18
Ht 09: Corradine, Bass, Robins, May	68.5	35 -19
Ht 10: Handley, Harding, Askew, Stratton	69.0	39 -21
Ht 11: Yeates, Young, Purkiss, Leonard	69.0	41 -25
Ht 12: Askew, Harding, Bass, Robins	69.0	45 -27
Ht 13: Yeates, Corradine, Leonard, Stratton	68.6	48 -30

OXFORD CHEETAHS v WEYMOUTH WIZARDS 22nd April 1976

Programme 16th April (one week earlier)

"Mick Handley is at present acting captain but here at Cowley we intend to break with tradition. Our team captain in future months will be the rider who attains the highest average on the official BSPA Green Sheets. These averages come out once a month. He will also ride as our No 1 Super Star. We are having specially made a Captain's No 1 and Super Star body colour for him to wear. So who will become the Cheetah's No 1 Super Star Captain for the first time?

We are very pleased to say the Cheetahs Supporters Club have very kindly offered to add a bonus to the points money our No 1 Super Star Captain gets during his reign."

SUPER STAR No 1 CAPTAIN: CARL ASKEW

Harry Bastable gives Carl Askew the Captain's vest in front of the home crowd.

CARL ASKEW

OXFORD CHEETAHS v WEYMOUTH WIZARDS 22nd April 1976

Carl Askew, Mick Handley, Brian Leonard

Heat 1: Carl Askew, Mick Handley, Martin Yeates, Gerald Purkiss

OXFORD CHEETAHS v WEYMOUTH WIZARDS 22nd April 1976

Heat 3: Mal Corradine, Phil Bass, Vic Harding and Roger Stratton

Mike Patrick, who made Cowley his homebase stadium in 1976, on the bend

LETTER TO THE OXFORD MAIL

COWLEY STADIUM REPORT

As there have been hints of pessimism in reports upon the progress at Cowley Stadium, I would like to state the situation after eight weeks of tenancy.

The crowds at speedway are expectedly down upon last year's figures, but the feeling is when people realise how exciting this new racing is we shall reach and even surpass that number.

At the moment, it is not just the crowd that is down, but the new promoters brought the prices down by including the programme in the admission price and also, I believe, reducing the car parking charge.

Greyhounds are now running three nights a week, Tuesday, Friday and Saturday and much money and effort have been put into preparing the dogtrack to a first class condition.

Stock cars run regularly throughout the summer and championship meetings are booked at Cowley for the first time.

A weekly market is held every Sunday morning at the Stadium and does a booming trade in every line from food to clothing.

Catering has been improved by bringing in outside firms offering a wider choice than before and meals are available in the clubhouse on greyhound nights.

After speedway meetings, for those who wish to have a whole evening out, there is a disco in the clubhouse with usually an extension to 11.30 p.m. and every Sunday evening live groups are booked at the club. Other events, including extra discos and cabarets are planned for future dates.

Once the main functions of the Stadium are well supported, it will be obvious that further entertainments are required and they will be provided.

The SOS Committee has been given two years to prove that Cowley Stadium is indispensable to the people of Oxford – obviously the people themselves must prove this. We have got the reprieve – the public must get the pardon.

Keith Lawson (SOS Committee)

SCUNTHORPE SAINTS v OXFORD CHEETAHS

26th April 1976

43-35

(National League)

Team Manager (Saints): Les Allum   Team Manager: Roger Jones

RIDERS INDIVIDUAL SCORE CHART														
SCUNTHORPE	**1**	**2**	**3**	**4**	**5**	**T**	**OXFORD**	**1**	**2**	**3**	**4**	**5**	**6**	**T**
1 Keith Evans	3	3	3	F	3	12	1 Carl Askew	1*	0	N	T			1
2 Sid Sheldrick(G)	0	0	0	1		1	2 Mal Corradine	2	2	1	0			5
3 Tony Childs						RR	3 Brian Leonard	0	2	0	1			3
4 Colin Cook	F	1	3	3	2*	9	4 Phil Bass	2	T	2*	1*			5
5 Andy Hines	3	3	X	2*	3	11	5 Kevin Young	1*	1	3	0			5
6 Ray Watkins	3	2*	2	2	1	10	6 Roy Sizmore	1*	1*	1				3
7 Tony Gillias	E	0	N	N		0	7 Mick Handley	2	1	3	3	2	2	13
8 Ian Silk	0					0								
						43								**35**

Ht 01: Evans, Corradine, Askew, Sheldrick   79.0   3 - 3

Ht 02: Watkins, Handley, Sizmore, Gillias (ef)   80.0   6 - 6

Ht 03: Hines, Bass, Young, Cook (f)   81.4   9 - 9

Ht 04: Evans, Watkins, Handley, Leonard   79.0   14 -10

Ht 05: Hines, Corradine, Cook, Askew   80.2   18 -12

Ht 06: Evans, Leonard, Sizmore, Sheldrick   78.6   21 -15

Ht 07: Handley, Watkins, Young, Gillias (ex 2 mins),   80.4   23 -19
             Bass (ex tapes)

Ht 08: Handley, Watkins, Corradine, Sheldrick   80.4   25 -23

Ht 09: Cook, Hines, Sizmore, Leonard   80.0   30 -24

Ht 10: Young, Bass, Sheldrick, Evans (f)   81.4   31 -29

Ht 11: Cook, Handley, Watkins, Corradine   80.2   35 -31

Ht 12: Evans, Cook, Leonard, Young   79.6   40 -32

Ht 13: Hines, Handley, Bass, Silk   79.4   43 -35

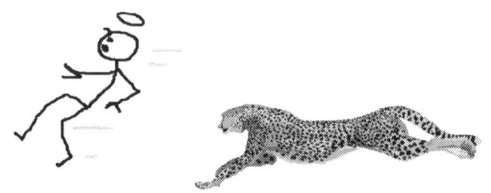

OXFORD CHEETAHS v WORKINGTON COMETS

29th April 1976

35-43

(National League)

Team Manager: Roger Jones   Team Manager (Comets): Alan Middleton

RIDERS INDIVIDUAL SCORE CHART													
OXFORD	**1**	**2**	**3**	**4**	**5**	**T**	**WORKINGTON**	**1**	**2**	**3**	**4**	**5**	**T**
1 Carl Askew	2	3	2	1		8	1 Steve Lawson	3	3	1	3	0	10
2 Kevin Young	0	0	1	0		1	2 Terry Kelly	1	3	2	1	0	7
3 Brian Leonard	1*	1	N	N		2	3 Lou Sansom	3	2	3	3	3	14
4 Phil Bass	1*	2	1*	0		4	4 Roger Wright						RR
5 Mal Corradine	2	0	N	1*		3	5 Colin Goad	0	2*	3	2*	3	10
6 Roy Sizmore	2*	2	0	1*		5	6 Chris Bevan	1	1*	0			2
7 Mick Handley	3	3	2	2	2	12	7 Stuart Collin	0	0	0			0
						35							**43**

Ht 01: Lawson, Askew, Kelly, Young	66.6	2 -4
Ht 02: Handley, Sizmore, Bevan, Collin	69.5	7 - 5
Ht 03: Lawson, Corradine, Bass, Goad	66.6	10 - 8
Ht 04: Sansom, Sizmore, Leonard, Collin **NL TR**	65.5	13 -11
Ht 05: Kelly, Bass, Lawson, Corradine	68.5	15 -15
Ht 06: Askew, Sansom, Bevan, Young	66.2	18 -18
Ht 07: Sansom, Goad, Leonard, Sizmore	66.6	19 -23
Ht 08: Handley, Kelly, Young, Collin	67.7	23 -25
Ht 09: Sansom, Handley, Bass, Bevan (f rem)	66.2	26 -28
Ht 10: Goad, Askew, Kelly, Young	67.6	28 -32
Ht 11: Lawson, Handley, Sizmore, Kelly	67.0	31 -35
Ht 12: Sansom, Goad, Askew, Bass	67.6	32 -40
Ht 13: Goad, Handley, Corradine, Lawson	67.4	35 -43

OXFORD CHEETAHS v WORKINGTON COMETS

Roger Jones' match report

"Well, although I was obviously disappointed in the result I'm sure the fans will agree it was very good racing. This was spearheaded on the Comet's side by their captain, Lou Sansom, and high-flying teenager Steve Lawson and, on the Cheetahs side by Mick Handley and Carl Askew.

Carl was involved in the most exciting race when, after the first lap was the length of the straight behind, was only second at the finishing line by a bike's length.

Full marks must go to Mick Handley, who rode brilliantly throughout the meeting – scoring 12 points -and topped it all by winning the second half final.

Roy Sizmore backed up Carl and Mick with another fine display from the reserve berth, although the rest of the team lacked a little determination.

Congratulations must go to the Comets, whose fine young rider, Steve Lawson, and experienced skipper, Lou Sansom, had a ding-dong battle for the track record, Lou coming off better, knocking 2 seconds off the previous record.

We feel that all the extra hard work put into the track last week accounted for the faster times – which are now drawing very close to those of last year's Gulf British League side."

Mick Handley's match report:

"Against Workington, we just couldn't get going. Mal was testing out a Weslake with very little success. Kev was plagued with clutch problems. The edge had gone off Phil's motor (he's ordered, and is patiently waiting for, a Crump/Street 4 valve) and I feel a couple of the lads were trying too hard. Self-confidence plays a very important and effort in one's riding is a thing that I can speak about from personal experience. If you try too hard, you can get all tied up inside and once this happens the rhythm of one's riding disappears."

COATBRIDGE TIGERS v OXFORD CHEETAHS

30th April 1976

40-38

Team Manager (Tigers): John Doherty   Team Manager: Roger Jones

RIDERS INDIVIDUAL SCORE CHART													
COATBRIDGE	1	2	3	4	5	T	OXFORD	1	2	3	4	5	T
1 Brian Collins	2*	2	2*	1	1*	8	1 Carl Askew	0	1	N	N		1
2 Jim Gallacher						RR	2 Kevin Young	1	3	1	0		5
3 Grahame Dawson	3	X	3	3	2	11	3 Brian Leonard	3	0	1	3		7
4 Mick McKeon	3	2	1*	2	2	10	4 Mal Corradine	1*	1	3	0		5
5 Doug Templeton	0	0	0	N		0	5 Phil Bass	2	0	2*	0		4
6 Rob Maxfield	2	1	2*	0		5	6 Mick Handley	3	3	3	2	3	14
7 Derek Richardson	1*	F	3	1	1*	6	7 Roy Sizmore	0	2*	0			2
						40							38

Ht 01: Dawson, Collins, Young, Askew (f rem)   71.4   5 - 1

Ht 02: Handley, Maxfield, Richardson, Sizmore   72.2   8 - 4

Ht 03: McKeon, Bass, Corradine, Templeton   73.2   11 - 7

Ht 04: Leonard, Sizmore, Maxfield, Richardson (f exc),   71.4   12 -12
                    Dawson (ex tapes)

Ht 05: Young, McKeon, Askew, Templeton   72.0   14 -16

Ht 06: Handley, Collins, McKeon, Leonard   71.8   17 -19

Ht 07: Dawson, Maxfield, Corradine, Bass   72.2   22 -20

Ht 08: Richardson, Collins, Young, Sizmore   72.4   27 -21

Ht 09: Handley, McKeon, Leonard, Templeton   72.2   29 -25

Ht 10: Corradine, Bass, Collins, Maxfield (f rem)   73.0   30 -30

Ht 11: Dawson, Handley, Richardson, Young   71.8   34 -32

Ht 12: Leonard, McKeon, Collins, Bass   72.8   37 -35

Ht 13: Handley, Dawson, Richardson, Corradine   72.4   40 -38

95

OXFORD CHEETAHS v NEWCASTLE DIAMONDS

6th May 1976

30-48

(National League)

Team Manager: Roger Jones   Team Manager (Diamonds): Dave Younghusband*

RIDERS INDIVIDUAL SCORE CHART													
OXFORD	1	2	3	4	5	T	NEWCASTLE	1	2	3	4	5	T
1 Carl Askew	3	1	2*	1		7	1 Tom Owen	F	1	3	3		7
2 Jim Wells	1	0	N	N		1	2 Ron Henderson	2	3	3	2*		10
3 Brian Leonard	0	0	T	0		0	3 Joe Owen	3	3	3	3		12
4 Phil Bass	3	2	0	1	0	6	4 Andy Cusworth	2	3	0	2*		7
5 Mal Corradine	1	0	X	1		2	5 Brian Havelock	0	1	1	2*		4
6 Mick Handley	3	2	2	0	3	10	6 Phil Michaelidies	0	2*	1			3
7 Roy Sizmore	1	1	2	0		4	Robbie Blackadder	2	1	2			5
						30							48

*some programmes say Ian Thomas, maybe the role was shared.

Ht 01: Askew, Henderson, Wells, T.Owen (f exc)   68.0   4 - 2

Ht 02: Handley, Blackadder, Sizmore, Michaelidies   70.5   8 - 4

Ht 03: Bass, Cusworth, Corradine, Havelock   69.0   12 - 6

Ht 04: J.Owen, Handley, Blackadder, Leonard   67.6   14 -10

Ht 05: Henderson, Bass, T.Owen, Corradine   68.5   16 -14

Ht 06: J.Owen, Michaelidies, Askew, Wells   67.8   17 -19

Ht 07: Cusworth, Handley, Havelock, Leonard   67.4   19 -23

Ht 08: Henderson, Blackadder, Sizmore, Handley   68.5   20 -28

Ht 09: J.Owen, Sizmore, Michaelidies, Bass, Corradine (tapes) 67.8   22 -32

Ht 10: Handley, Askew, Havelock, Cusworth   68.0   27 -33

Ht 11: T.Owen, Henderson, Bass, Sizmore   67.5   28 -38

Ht 12: J.Owen, Havelock, Askew, Bass   67.4   29 -43

Ht 13: T.Owen, Cusworth, Corradine, Leonard   67.5   30 -48

Jim Wells make his debut as a Cheetah (having tried out in last week's second half) and happy to sign a contract. NB this would be Jim's final year in UK speedway.

OXFORD CHEETAHS v NEWCASTLE DIAMONDS

Jim Wells

Roy Sizmore

OXFORD CHEETAHS v NEWCASTLE DIAMONDS

Joe Owen

Tom Owen

OXFORD CHEETAHS v NEWCASTLE DIAMONDS

Ron Henderson

OXFORD CHEETAHS v NEWCASTLE DIAMONDS

Robbie Blackadder

Phil Michaelidies

Andy Cusworth

Brian Havelock

OXFORD CHEETAHS v NEWCASTLE DIAMONDS

Heat 1: Ron Henderson, Tom Owen, Carl Askew and Jim Wells

Heat 1: Tom Owen falls (excluded) bringing down Carl Askew

OXFORD CHEETAHS v NEWCASTLE DIAMONDS

Heat 1: Tom Owen down

Heat 1: Carl Askew taken out by Tom Owen's spill

OXFORD CHEETAHS v NEWCASTLE DIAMONDS

Heat 1: (rerun) Ron Henderson and Carl Askew

Heat 2: Roy Sizmore and Mick Handley

OXFORD CHEETAHS v NEWCASTLE DIAMONDS

Heat 3: Brian Havelock and Phil Bass

Heat 4: Joe Owen

OXFORD CHEETAHS v NEWCASTLE DIAMONDS

Heat 4: Joe Owen and Brian Leonard

Heat 4: Joe Owen

PETERBOROUGH PANTHERS v OXFORD CHEETAHS

7th May 1976

24-12

(National League)

Team Manager (Panthers): Ron Orchard   Team Manager: Roger Jones

RIDERS INDIVIDUAL SCORE CHART													
PETERBOROUGH	**1**	**2**	**3**	**4**	**5**	**T**	**OXFORD**	**1**	**2**	**3**	**4**	**5**	**T**
1 Tony Featherstone	3	2				5	1 Carl Askew	1	2				3
2 Roy Carter	2*	1*				3	2 Jim Wells	0	0				0
3 Brian Clark	E					0	3 Brian Leonard						RR
4 Ken Matthews	3	3				6	4 Phil Bass	0					0
5 Alan Cowland	1	1				2	5 Mal Corradine	2	3				5
6 Steve Taylor	2*	3				5	6 Mick Handley	1	2	0			3
7 Ian Clark	3					3	7 Roy Sizmore	F	1*				1
						24							12

Ht 01: Featherstone, Carter, Askew, Wells   70.2   5 - 1

Ht 02: I.Clark, Taylor, Handley, Sizmore (f exc)   69.2   10 - 2

Ht 03: Matthews, Corradine, Cowland, Bass   70.6   14 - 4

Ht 04: Taylor, Handley, Sizmore, B.Clark (ef)   71.0   17 - 7

Ht 05: Matthews, Askew, Cowland, Wells   72.0   21 - 9

Ht 06: Corradine, Featherstone, Carter, Handley   No Time   24 -12

Meeting Abandoned Due To Power Failure- Result Does Not Stand !

From the stands we saw a lightning strike hit the ground in the distance. Apparently it hit a substation as the power went out.

What was worse? No racing, or no power for the beer pumps in the stadium bar? At least it saved the Cheetahs from a massacre.

NB this might the meeting when Mal Corradine got butted by a goat while walking from the changing rooms to the pits, a story told me by Carl Askew. [Peterborough track was the Count Showground.]

OXFORD MAIL NEWS

11th May 1976

STADIUM DISCOS CUT AS MANAGER GOES

Cowley Stadium has sacked its entertainments manager.

Mr Tony Dell, the radio disc jockey and actor, has been given notice in an attempt by the stadium to save money.

He said, "It was a shock to find myself redundant at such short notice. When I first started it was with the aim of making the club at the stadium the city's premier place of entertainment."

A spokesman for the stadium management said that the profits made from Mr Dell's efforts did not justify his continued employment.

The weekday discotheques will no longer be held at the stadium club apart from those run by the speedway promoters. Groups will still perform on Sundays.

Picture shows Tony Dell having a drink with Radio 1 DJ, Emperor Rosko, in 1976.

Tony continued to live at the White Buffalo that year before moving away. I last saw him in "Auf Wiedersehn, Pet" (the Spanish season).

OXFORD CHEETAHS v EASTBOURNE EAGLES

13th May 1976

47-31

(National League KOC 1st Round 1st Leg)

Team Manager: Roger Jones   Team Manager (Eagles): Arthur Nutley

OXFORD	1	2	3	4	5	T	EASTBOURNE	1	2	3	4	5	T
RIDERS INDIVIDUAL SCORE CHART													
1 Carl Askew	2	2*	1	3		8	1 Steve Weatherley	3	3	3	3	3	15
2 Brian Leonard	F	3	2	3		8	2 Colin Richardson	1	0	0	1		2
3 Mick Handley	3	0	2	2		7	3 Mike Sampson	1	1	0	1		3
4 Kevin Young	1*	1*	N	N		2	4 Pete Jarman	0	1*	0	0		1
5 Mal Corradine	2	2	1	1*		6	5 Eric Dugard	3	2	2	2	0	9
6 Phil Bass	3	2*	3	3	2	13	6 Steve Naylor	F	0	T			0
7 Roy Sizmore	2*	1*	F			3	7 Roger Abel	1	0	T			1
						47							31

Ht 01: Weatherley, Askew, Richardson, Leonard (f)	66.6	2 - 4
Ht 02: Bass, Sizmore, Abel, Naylor (f)	68.0	7 - 5
Ht 03: Dugard, Corradine, Young, Jarman	67.3	10 - 8
Ht 04: Handley, Bass, Sampson, Abel	69.0	15 - 9
Ht 05: Weatherley, Corradine, Young, Richardson	66.0	18 -12
Ht 06: Leonard, Askew, Sampson, Naylor	67.8	23 -13
Ht 07: Bass, Dugard, Jarman, Handley	68.2	26 -16
Ht 08: Weatherley, Leonard, Sizmore, Richardson	66.4	29 -19
Ht 09: Bass, Dugard, Corradine, Sampson	68.1	33 -21
Ht 10: Leonard, Dugard, Askew, Jarman	67.2	37 -23
Ht 11: Weatherley, Handley, Richardson, Sizmore (f)	66.2	39 -27
Ht 12: Askew, Bass, Sampson, Dugard	68.2	44 -28
Ht 13: Weatherley, Handley, Corradine, Jarman	66.4	47 -31

EASTBOURNE EAGLES v OXFORD CHEETAHS

16th May 1976

41-37

(National League KOC 1st Round 2nd Leg)

Team Manager (Eagles): Arthur Nutley   Team Manager: Roger Jones

RIDERS INDIVIDUAL SCORE CHART													
EASTBOURNE	1	2	3	4	5	T	OXFORD	1	2	3	4	5	T
1 Steve Weatherley	3	3	2	3		11	1 Carl Askew	1*	2	2*	2	3	10
2 Colin Richardson	0	1	1	1*		3	2 Kevin Young	2	0	T	F	0	2
3 Mike Sampson	3	3	3	1		10	3 Mick Handley	E	2	3	3	2	10
4 Eric Dugard	2	3	2	0		7	4 Brian Leonard	3	2	3	1*	2*	11
5 Pete Jarman	F	1	1*	N		2	5 Mal Corradine	1	F	0	T		1
6 Colin Ackroyd	2*	1	N			3	6 Phil Bass	0	0	T			0
7 Steve Naylor	3	1	0	1	0	5	7 Roy Sizmore	1	2	T			3
						41							37

Agg: Oxford 84 - 72 Eastbourne

Ht 01: Weatherley, Young, Askew, Richardson   62.4   3 - 3

Ht 02: Naylor, Ackroyd, Sizmore, Bass   63.8   8 - 4

Ht 03: Leonard, Dugard, Corradine, Jarman (f exc)   62.4   10 - 8

Ht 04: Sampson, Sizmore, Ackroyd, Handley (ef)   64.0   14 -10

Ht 05: Dugard, Askew, Jarman, Young   62.6   18 -12

Ht 06: Weatherley, Handley, Richardson, Bass   62.2   22 -14

Ht 07: Sampson, Leonard, Naylor, Corradine (f)   64.2   26 -16

Ht 08: Handley, Askew, Richardson, Naylor (f rem)   64.6   27 -21

Ht 09: Handley, Dugard, Jarman, Young (f exc)   63.0   30 -24

Ht 10: Leonard, Weatherley, Richardson, Corradine   63.0   33 -27

Ht 11: Sampson, Askew, Naylor, Young   63.8   37 -29

Ht 12: Weatherley, Handley, Leonard, Dugard   63.0   40 -32

Ht 13: Askew, Leonard, Sampson, Naylor (f rem)   64.8   41 -37

Taking photos of the racing was a problem – the dust and reflection made it difficult to take accurate light readings and set up the exposure. We photographers had to work at our art back then - we didn't have today's computers with lens attached aka digital cameras - and would have to adjust constantly for changes in the light.

Carl Askew

Phil Bass

EASTBOURNE EAGLES v OXFORD CHEETAHS

Roy Sizmore

Mick Handley

Eric Dugard

Colin Richardson

Colin Ackroyd

Mike Sampson

Pete Jarman

EASTBOURNE EAGLES v OXFORD CHEETAHS

Dave Lanning

Kevin Young, Brian Leonard (standing), Mick Handley, Phil Bass, Roy Sizmore

Carl Askew

EASTBOURNE EAGLES v OXFORD CHEETAHS

Heat 1: Carl Askew leads Colin Richardson

EASTBOURNE EAGLES v OXFORD CHEETAHS

Heat 1: Steve Weatherley and Carl Askew

Heat 2: Steve Naylor. Phil Bass (w), Colin Ackroyd, Roy Sizmore

EASTBOURNE EAGLES v OXFORD CHEETAHS

Heat 2: Phil Bass (w), Colin Ackroyd, Roy Sizmore

Heat 3: Brian Leonard and Eric Dugard

Heat 3: Brian Leonard and Eric Dugard

Heat 3: Brian Leonard, Mal Corradine, Eric Dugard, Pete Jarman

Heat 3: Brian Leonard, Mal Corradine, Eric Dugard,

Heat 3: Brian Leonard's wheel, Eric Dugard, Mal Corradine, and Pete Jarman

Heat 4: Roy Sizmore, Colin Ackroyd, Phil Bass, and Mike Sampson

Heat 5: Kevin Young (yb) Pete Jarman, Eric Dugard

Heat 6: Colin Richardson and Phil Bass (yb)

Heat 6: Phil Bass (yb) and Mick Handley (w)

Heat 8: Carl Askew and Steve Naylor

Heat 8: Mick Handley, Colin Richardson, and Carl Askew

Heat 9: Eric Dugard and Kevin Young (falling)

EASTBOURNE EAGLES v OXFORD CHEETAHS   16th May 1976

Heat 9: Mick Handley, Eric Dugard, and Pete Jarman

Kevin Young and Carl Askew

Mick Handley

EASTBOURNE EAGLES v OXFORD CHEETAHS   16th May 1976

Roy Sizmore

Brian Leonard nearest (this might be a second half race)
I think that is Cheetahs promoter Tony Allsopp behind the fence.

Steve Weatherley

EASTBOURNE EAGLES v OXFORD CHEETAHS   16th May 1976

A great coach outing, with some riders travelling down with the fans and others joining us for a group photo at Eastbourne (below).

The usual suspects LOL

Great camaraderie between travelling fans and the riders.
My big regret is that I am not in the photo!

Harry Bastable, Mick Handley, Carl Askew, Mal Corradine, Phil Bass, Kevin Young, Ann Cross (now Booker), Bernard Crapper, Keith Pilcher (and his wife), Mick 'Foreman' Harris, Roger Jones, Norman Hunter, Ian Roberts, Adrian Cross, 'Pop', and all the faces I remember (but not all the names).

I bet this has never been done before or since – a unique moment in any club's history.

OXFORD: ARTDEANS BEST PAIRS TROPHY   20th May 1976
Meeting postponed due to rain

OXFORD CHEETAHS v COATBRIDGE TIGERS

27th May 1976

49-29

(National League)

Team Manager: Roger Jones   Team Manager (Tigers): John Doherty

RIDERS INDIVIDUAL SCORE CHART														
OXFORD	**1**	**2**	**3**	**4**	**5**	**T**	**COATBRIDGE**	**1**	**2**	**3**	**4**	**5**	**6**	**T**
1 Carl Askew	3	2*	3	2*		10	1 Brian Collins	1*	2	2	3	3	2	13
2 Kevin Young	0	3	1	0		4	2 Derek Richardson	2	1*	2*	1*	0	0	6
3 Mick Handley	3	2*	2	3		10	3 Grahame Dawson	0	0	T	T			0
4Brian Leonard	3	3	2	3		11	4 Jim Gallacher							RR
5 Jim Wells	1	0	1*	1		3	5 Rob Maxfield	0	1	N	0			1
6 Phil Bass	3	2*	3			8	6 Doug Templeton	0	N	E				0
7 Roy Sizmore	2*	0	1			3	7 Mick McKeon	1	1	1	3	2	1	9
							8 John Wilson	0						0
						49								**29**

Ht 01: Askew, Richardson, Collins, Young   68.0   3 - 3

Ht 02: Bass, Sizmore, McKeon, Templeton   68.2   8 - 4

Ht 03: Leonard, Collins, Wells, Maxfield   67.4   12 - 6

Ht 04: Handley, Bass, McKeon, Dawson   68.5   17 - 7

Ht 05: Leonard, Collins, Richardson, Wells   67.2   20 -10

Ht 06: Young, Askew, McKeon, Dawson   68.7   25 -11

Ht 07: Bass, Handley, Maxfield, Wilson   68.8   30 -12

Ht 08: McKeon, Richardson, Young, Sizmore   69.0   31 -17

Ht 09: Collins, Leonard, Wells, Templeton (ef)   67.5   34 -20

Ht 10: Askew, McKeon, Richardson, Young   69.0   37 -23

Ht 11: Collins, Handley, Sizmore, Richardson (f rem)   67.8   40 -26

Ht 12: Leonard, Askew, McKeon, Maxfield   66.9   45 -27

Ht 13: Handley, Collins, Wells, Richardson   68.1   49 -29

BOSTON BARRACUDAS v OXFORD CHEETAHS

30ᵗʰ May 1976

40-37

(National League)

Team Manager (Barracudas):   Team Manager: Roger Jones

RIDERS INDIVIDUAL SCORE CHART													
BOSTON	**1**	**2**	**3**	**4**	**5**	**T**	**OXFORD**	**1**	**2**	**3**	**4**	**5**	**T**
1 Billy Burton	3	3	2	F		8	1 Carl Askew	2	2	2	X		6
2 Stuart Cope	1	1	0	F		2	2 Brian Leonard	E	1*	2*	1*		4
3 Rob Hollingworth	3	3	3	3		12	3 Mick Handley	2	0	0	X		2
4 Paul Gilbert	3	3	2	2		10	4 Kevin Young	2	1*	3	2		8
5 Trevor Whiting	F	0	N	N		0	5 Jim Wells	1*	2	X	3		6
6 Ron Cooper	3	1	0	1*	1*	6	6 Phil Bass	2	2	3	3	X	10
7 Steve Clarke	0	1	0	1		2	7 Andy Bales(G)	1*	F	N			1
						40							**37**

Ht 01: Burton, Askew, Cope, Leonard (ef)   66.4   4 - 2

Ht 02: Cooper, Bass, Bales, Clarke   67.8   7 - 5

Ht 03: Gilbert, Young, Wells, Whiting (f)   66.4   10 - 8

Ht 04: Hollingworth, Handley, Cooper, Bales (f)   66.0   14 -10

Ht 05: Gilbert, Askew, Leonard, Whiting   66.8   17 -13

Ht 06: Burton, Bass, Cope, Handley   66.6   21 -15

Ht 07: Hollingworth, Wells, Young, Cooper   No Time   24 -18

Ht 08: Bass, Leonard, Clarke, Cope   67.4   25 -23

Ht 09: Bass, Gilbert, Cooper, Handley   66.8   28 -26

Ht 10: Young, Burton, Cooper, Wells (ex boring),   66.8   31 -29
        Cope (f ns)

Ht 11: Hollingworth, Askew, Leonard, Clarke   66.2   34 -32

Ht 12: Wells, Gilbert (ef pushed), Bass (ex tapes),   67.0   36 -35
        Burton (f exc), Handley (ex tapes)

Ht 13: Hollingworth, Young, Clarke, Bass (ef),   66.4   40 -37
        Askew (ex tapes)

ELLESMERE PORT GUNNERS v OXFORD CHEETAHS

1st June 1976

51-27

(Thames-Mersey Trophy 1st Leg)

Team Manager (Gunners): Joe Shaw   Team Manager: Roger Jones

RIDERS INDIVIDUAL SCORE CHART													
ELLESMERE	1	2	3	4	5	T	OXFORD	1	2	3	4	5	T
1 John Jackson	3	3	3	3		12	1 Carl Askew	2	2	3	1	1	9
2 Gerald Smitherman	1	1	2	F		4	2 Kevin Young	0	1*	T	1*	0	2
3 Chris Turner	3	3	3	3		12	3 Mick Handley	0	0	1	N		1
4 Robbie Gardner	3	E	2*	E		5	4 Jim Wells	0	0	T	0		0
5 Steve Finch	2*	3	3	2*		10	5 Brian Leonard	1	1	2	2		6
6 Duncan Meredith	3	N	2*	2*		7	6 Phil Bass	2	2	0	1*		5
7 Louis Carr	X	1	0	N		1	7 Roy Sizmore	1*	2	1			4
								51					27

Ht 01: Jackson, Askew, Smitherman, Young	74.4	4 - 2
Ht 02: Meredith, Bass, Sizmore, Carr (exc)	76.2	7 - 5
Ht 03: Gardner, Finch, Leonard, Wells	75.2	12 - 6
Ht 04: Turner, Sizmore, Carr, Handley	77.0	16 - 8
Ht 05: Finch, Askew, Young, Gardner (ef)	76.8	19 -11
Ht 06: Jackson, Bass, Smitherman, Handley	75.0	23 -13
Ht 07: Turner, Meredith, Leonard, Wells	76.5	28 -14
Ht 08: Askew, Smitherman, Sizmore, Carr	77.4	30 -18
Ht 09: Finch, Gardner, Handley, Bass	77.4	35 -19
Ht 10: Jackson, Leonard, Young, Smitherman (f exc)	76.2	38 -22
Ht 11: Turner, Meredith, Askew, Young	76.8	43 -23
Ht 12: Jackson, Leonard, Bass, Gardner (ef)	76.6	46 -26
Ht 13: Turner, Finch, Askew, Wells	77.6	52 -27

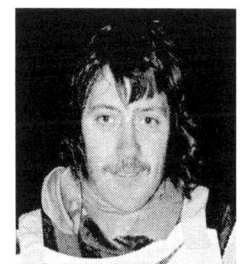

Gerald Smitherman

OXFORD CHEETAHS v ELLESMERE PORT GUNNERS

3rd June 1976

36-42

(Thames-Mersey Trophy 2nd Leg)

Team Manager: Roger Jones   Team Manager (Gunners): Joe Shaw

RIDERS INDIVIDUAL SCORE CHART														
OXFORD	1	2	3	4	5	6	T	**ELLESMERE**	1	2	3	4	5	T
1 Carl Askew	1*	1	2*	2			6	1 John Jackson	3	3	3	3		12
2 Kevin Young	2	0	3	3			8	2 Gerald Smitherman	0	1	0	1		2
3 Mick Handley	1	3	2	2			8	3 Chris Turner	2	3	3	3		11
4Brian Leonard	0	2	1	N			3	4 Robbie Gardner	2*	0	1	1		4
5 Jim Wells	1	0	0	N			1	5 Steve Finch	3	1	0	0		4
6 Phil Bass	E	3	2*	2*	1	0	8	6 Duncan Meredith	3	2*	1	2*		8
7 Steve Holden	2	T	O				2	7 Phil Collins	1	0	N			1
							36							42

Agg: Ellesmere Port 93 - 63 Oxford

Ht 01: Jackson, Young, Askew, Smitherman   67.0   3 - 3

Ht 02: Meredith, Holden, Collins, Bass (ef)   68.2   5 - 7

Ht 03: Finch, Gardner, Wells, Leonard   68.4   6 -12

Ht 04: Bass, Turner, Handley, Collins   67.4   10 -14

Ht 05: Jackson, Leonard, Smitherman, Wells   67.6   12 -18

Ht 06: Turner, Meredith, Askew, Young   67.7   13 -23

Ht 07: Handley, Bass, Finch, Gardner   67.5   18 -24

Ht 08: Young, Bass, Meredith, Smitherman   68.4   23 -25

Ht 09: Turner, Meredith, Leonard, Wells   68 1   24 -30

Ht 10: Young, Askew, Gardner, Finch   68.0   29 -31

Ht 11: Jackson, Handley, Smitherman, Holden   67.5   31 -35

Ht 12: Turner, Askew, Bass, Finch   67.6   34 -38

Ht 13: Jackson, Handley, Gardner, Bass   67.0   36 -42

OXFORD CHEETAHS v ELLESMERE PORT GUNNERS

3rd June 1976

Roger Jones' report:

"Although we are obviously disappointed at losing the Mersey-Thames Trophy, we would like to congratulate the Ellesmere Port Gunners for providing such an entertaining match.

Carl, Mick, Phil and Kevin all pout up very spirited performances, but the might of John Jackson, Chris Turner and Duncan Meredith was too much.

One could say that, with Phil Bass's bike troubles, we were unlucky not to win the second leg but, firstly, we don't make excuses when we lose to a better side than us and, secondly, Phil got his own back in the second half final.

After his performance, Steve Holden's future at Oxford seems very doubtful. Although we won't throw him out, unless he pulls his socks up we could put him up for transfer.

Pip Lamb was a good source of interest and has earned himself an extended run in the second half. We have decided to offer him a contract to ride for the Cheetahs and, in view of his continuing progress, we are also watching Kevin Hawkins very carefully."

Pip Lamb

RYE HOUSE ROCKETS v OXFORD CHEETAHS

6th June 1976

46-32

(National League)

Team Manager (Rockets): Colin Pratt   Team Manager: Roger Jones

RIDERS INDIVIDUAL SCORE CHART													
RYE HOUSE	1	2	3	4	5	T	OXFORD	1	2	3	4	5	T
1 Brian Foote	2	1	1	0		4	1 Carl Askew	3	2	2	2	F	9
2 Kelvin Mullarkey	1*	3	3	R		7	2 Roy Sizmore	0	0	T	T		0
3 Hugh Saunders	2*	1*	3	3		9	3 Mick Handley	1	R	R	N		1
4 Karl Fiala	2*	3	3	2		10	4 Jim Wells	0	R	2*	2		4
5 Ted Hubbard	3	1	2*	F		6	5 Phil Bass	1	3	3	1*	3	11
6 Bob Garrad	3	3	2	1		9	6 Brian Leonard	2	2	1	1		6
7 Ashley Pullen	1	F	0			1	7 Kevin Young	0	0	1*			1
						46							32

Ht 01: Askew, Foote, Mullarkey, Sizmore	64.0	3 - 3
Ht 02: Garrad, Leonard, Pullen, Young	64.6	7 - 5
Ht 03: Hubbard, Fiala, Bass, Wells	62.6	12 - 6
Ht 04: Garrad, Saunders, Handley, Young	63.6	17 - 7
Ht 05: Fiala, Askew, Hubbard, Sizmore	64.2	21 - 9
Ht 06: Mullarkey, Leonard, Foote, Handley (ret)	64.4	25 -11
Ht 07: Bass, Garrad, Saunders, Wells (ret)	64.4	28 -14
Ht 08: Mullarkey, Askew, Young, Pullen (f)	64.2	31 -17
Ht 09: Fiala, Hubbard, Leonard, Handley (ret)	64.2	36 -18
Ht 10: Bass, Wells, Foote, Mullarkey (ret)	65.0	37 -23
Ht 11: Saunders, Askew, Bass, Pullen	64.6	40 -26
Ht 12: Bass, Fiala, Leonard, Foote	64.4	42 -30
Ht 13: Saunders, Wells, Garrad, Askew (f exc),	65.4	46 -32
Hubbard (f ns)		

Heat 10: Brian Foote, Phil Bass (w) and Kelvin Mullarkey

Heat 11: Hugh Saunders, Phil Bass and Carl Askew

Heat 11: Hugh Saunders, Phil Bass and Carl Askew

Phil Bass

OXFORD CHEETAHS v RYE HOUSE ROCKETS

10th June 1976

39-39

(National League)

Team Manager: Roger Jones   Team Manager (Rockets): Colin Pratt

RIDERS INDIVIDUAL SCORE CHART													
OXFORD	1	2	3	4	5	T	RYE HOUSE	1	2	3	4	5	T
1 Carl Askew	2	3	3	2	3	13	1 Brian Foote	3	1	0	N		4
2 Roy Sizmore	1*	1	T	0		2	2 Kelvin Mullarkey	0	3	1*	2		6
3 Mick Handley	0	0	N	N		0	3 Hugh Saunders	3	2	0	0		5
4 Jim Wells	1	0	N	N		1	4 Karl Fiala	2*	1*	1	2		6
5 Phil Bass	0	2	1	3		6	5 Ted Hubbard	3	2	3	1		9
6 Brian Leonard	2	2	3	3	1	11	6 Ashley Pullen	0	0	N			0
7 Kevin Young	1*	0	3	2*	0	6	7 Bob Garrad	3	1	2	2	1*	9
						39							39

Ht 01: Foote, Askew, Sizmore, Mullarkey   66.8   3 - 3

Ht 02: Garrad, Leonard, Young, Pullen (f rem)   66.2   6 - 6

Ht 03: Hubbard, Fiala, Wells, Bass   66.9   7 -11

Ht 04: Saunders, Leonard, Garrad, Handley   66.3   9 -15

Ht 05: Mullarkey, Bass, Foote, Wells   67.2   11 -19

Ht 06: Askew, Saunders, Sizmore, Pullen   (NL TR)   65.4   15 -21

Ht 07: Leonard, Hubbard, Fiala, Handley   67.6   18 -24

Ht 08: Askew, Garrad, Mullarkey, Young   66.5   21 -27

Ht 09: Leonard, Garrad, Bass, Saunders   67.0   25 -29

Ht 10: Hubbard, Askew, Fiala, Sizmore   66.9   27 -33

Ht 11: Young, Mullarkey, Leonard, Foote   67.2   31 -35

Ht 12: Askew, Young, Hubbard, Saunders   67.4   36 -36

Ht 13: Bass, Fiala, Garrad, Young   66.9   39 -39

Jim Wells finally got his own bike for this meeting.

Mal Corradine was to miss all the Away matches so it was under consideration whether it was time to part company.

Harry MacLean would be out for an expected six weeks,possibly needing an operation on his arm.

Kevin Young and Phil Bass had 4 valve conversions to their bikes.

OXFORD CHEETAHS v RYE HOUSE ROCKETS

Heat 2: Ashley Pullen, Brian Leonard and (at back) Kevin Young

Heat 3: Karl Fiala (yb),Phil Bass, Jim Wells, Ted Hubbard

RYE HOUSE ROCKETS

The photos are from 1977 but I want to say something about these guys.

Ashley Pullen

I first knew Ashley when he was a "rug rat" - his brother, Ian, and I were classmates for 5 years at Oxford High School.
The family lived only half a mile from the stadium. My first taste of journalism was with Ian, running the class magazine.

Karl Fiala is the Mr Speedway of Facebook, his group "Speedway Friends" is the one to join for a broad range of speedway news and memories.

https://www.facebook.com/groups/198832456794185/?ref=bookmarks

Karl Fiala

CANTERBURY CRUSADERS v OXFORD CHEETAHS

12th June 1976

53-25

(National League)

Team Manager (Crusaders):   Team Manager: Roger Jones

RIDERS INDIVIDUAL SCORE CHART													
CANTERBURY	**1**	**2**	**3**	**4**	**5**	**T**	**OXFORD**	**1**	**2**	**3**	**4**	**5**	**T**
1 Les Rumsey	3	3	3	2*		11	1 Carl Askew	1	2	0	N		3
2 Steve Koppe	2*	2*	1	1		6	2 Roy Sizmore	0	1*	2	1		4
3 Barney Kennett	3	2	2*	3		10	3 Mick Handley	2	0	0	0		2
4 Terry Casserly	1	0	1*	3		5	4 Phil Bass	2	3	3	2	2	12
5 Reg Luckhurst	3	3	2	N		8	5 Jim Wells	0	0	0	1		1
6 Bob Spelta	2*	0	1*			3	6 Brian Leonard	1	1	T			2
7 Graham Banks	3	3	3	1		10	7 Kevin Young	0	1*	0	0		1
						53							**25**

Ht 01: Rumsey, Koppe, Askew, Sizmore   73.0   5 - 1

Ht 02: Banks, Spelta, Leonard, Young   73.2   10 - 2

Ht 03: Luckhurst, Bass, Casserly, Wells   72.6   14 - 4

Ht 04: Kennett, Handley, Young, Spelta   73.2   17 - 7

Ht 05: Luckhurst, Askew, Sizmore, Casserly   73.8   20 -10

Ht 06: Rumsey, Koppe, Leonard, Handley   73.6   25 -11

Ht 07: Bass, Kennett, Spelta, Wells   72.6   28 -14

Ht 08: Banks, Sizmore, Koppe, Young   73.0   32 -16

Ht 09: Bass, Luckhurst, Casserly, Handley   72.8   35 -19

Ht 10: Rumsey, Bass, Koppe, Wells   72.0   39 -21

Ht 11: Banks, Kennett, Sizmore, Askew   74.2   44 -22

Ht 12: Casserly, Rumsey, Wells, Handley   72.4   49 -23

Ht 13: Kennett, Bass, Banks, Young   72.6   53 -25

OXFORD CHEETAHS v STOKE POTTERS

17th June 1976

50-27

(National League)

Team Manager: Roger Jones   Team Manager (Potters): Chris Harrison

RIDERS INDIVIDUAL SCORE CHART													
OXFORD	**1**	**2**	**3**	**4**	**5**	**T**	**STOKE**	**1**	**2**	**3**	**4**	**5**	**T**
1 Carl Askew	3	3	3	1		10	1 Les Collins	2	2	1*	3		11
2 Roy Sizmore	0	0	N	N		0	2 Jim Brett	1*	0	1	1		2
3 Mick Handley	3	2*	0	2		7	3 Ricky Day	1*	2	1	2		6
4 Brian Leonard	3	3	3	3		12	4 Jack Millen	1	E	F	0		1
5 Phil Bass	2*	1	2*	1*		6	5 Tim Nunan	0	1	F	0		1
6 Mal Corradine	E	E	3	3		6	6 Andy Reid	2	T	E			2
7 Kevin Young	3	2*	2*	2		9	7 Neil Webb	1*	2	R			3
						50							**27**

Ht 01: Askew, Collins, Brett, Sizmore   66.8   3 - 3

Ht 02: Young, Reid, Webb, Corradine (ef)   68.5   6 - 6

Ht 03: Leonard, Bass, Millen, Nunan   67.6   11 - 7

Ht 04: Handley, Webb, Day, Corradine (ef)   68.6   14 -10

Ht 05: Leonard, Collins, Bass, Brett   67.1   18 -12

Ht 06: Askew, Day, Collins, Sizmore   67.5   21 -15

Ht 07: Corradine, Handley, Nunan, Millen (ef)   68.4   26 -16

Ht 08: Corradine, Young, Brett, Webb (f)   68.2   31 -17

Ht 09: Leonard, Bass, Day, Reid (ef)   68.1   36 -18

Ht 10: Askew, Young, Millen (f exc),   69.2   41 -18

      Nunan (f exc)

Ht 11: Collins, Young, Brett, Handley   67.0   43 -22

Ht 12: Leonard, Day, Askew, Nunan   67.5   47 -24

Ht 13: Collins, Handley, Bass, Brett   67.2   50 -27

Phil Bass

152

OXFORD CHEETAHS v STOKE POTTERS

Roger Jones' report:

"What a tremendous match this turned out to be. The Cheetahs turned out a fabulous performance, which sent the Potters reeling back on their proverbial heels. Tony and Harry's old promotion came to Oxford with every intention of gaining two league points, but the Cheetahs, led brilliantly by return-to-form man, Brian Leonard, certainly removed all their hopes.

Carl Askew put up another sturdy performance, while Kevin Young was flying in the reserve berth.

It was pleasing to see Mal Corradine returning to the side, although he was unlucky with bike troubles.

Mick Handley seems to have lost his bike 'jinx' and turned out his best performance for some time."

Kevin Young

STOKE POTTERS v OXFORD CHEETAHS 19th June 1976

Meeting postponed due to rain

BOSTON BARRACUDAS v OXFORD CHEETAHS

20th June 1976

41-36

(Revenge Challenge)

Team Manager (Barracudas):   Team Manager: Roger Jones

RIDERS INDIVIDUAL SCORE CHART													
BOSTON	1	2	3	4	5	T	**OXFORD**	1	2	3	4	5	T
1 Billy Burton	3	2	2	3		10	1 Carl Askew	1*	2	1	N		4
2 Paul Gilbert	0	1*	2	1*		4	2 Roy Sizmore	2	1*	1	N		4
3 Rob Hollingworth	2	3	3	3	3	14	3 Mick Handley	1	0	N	0		1
4 Stuart Cope	1	0	T	2*		3	4 Phil Bass	3	2	3	1*		9
5 Trevor Whiting	0	3	2*	0		5	5 Brian Leonard	2*	1*	0	1		4
6 Steve Clarke	3	0	0			3	6 Mal Corradine	E	3	1	X		4
7 Ron Cooper	F	F	2*			2	7 Kevin Young	2	3	3	0	2	10
						41							**36**

Ht 01: Burton, Sizmore, Askew, Gilbert   69.0   3 - 3

Ht 02: Clarke, Young, Cooper (f), Corradine (ef)   67.6   6 - 5

Ht 03: Bass, Leonard, Cope, Whiting   68.0   7 -10

Ht 04: Young, Hollingworth, Handley, Clarke   67.8   9 -14

Ht 05: Whiting, Askew, Sizmore, Cope   67.2   12 -17

Ht 06: Corradine, Burton, Gilbert, Handley   67.4   15 -20

Ht 07: Hollingworth, Bass, Leonard, Clarke (f rem)   66.8   18 -23

Ht 08: Young, Gilbert, Sizmore, Cooper (f)   67.0   20 -27

Ht 09: Hollingworth, Whiting, Corradine, Young   65.8   25 -28

Ht 10: Bass, Burton, Gilbert, Leonard   66.2   28 -31

Ht 11: Hollingworth, Cooper, Askew, Corradine (exc)   65.4   33 -32

Ht 12: Burton, Cope, Leonard, Handley   66.4   38 -33

Ht 13: Hollingworth, Young, Bass, Whiting   65.8   41 -36

OXFORD CHEETAHS v CRAYFORD KESTRELS

24th June 1976

42-36

(National League)

Team Manager: Roger Jones   Team Manager (Kestrels): Peter Thorogood

RIDERS INDIVIDUAL SCORE CHART													
OXFORD	**1**	**2**	**3**	**4**	**5**	**T**	**CRAYFORD**	**1**	**2**	**3**	**4**	**5**	**T**
1 Carl Askew	1	3	3	3		10	1 Laurie Etheridge	3	3	3	2	3	14
2 Roy Sizmore	0	1	2	0		3	2 Pete Wigley						RR
3 Mick Handley	3	2	3	2		10	3 Alan Sage	2*	2	2	2	2	10
4 Brian Leonard	1	1*	3	1		6	4 Mike Broadbank	2	0	3	1*	0	6
5 Phil Bass	3	2	1	1*		7	5 Alan Johns	F	E	2	1*	F	3
6 Mal Corradine	2*	E	1*			3	6 Gary Spencer	1	0	0			1
7 Kevin Young	3	0	0			3	7 John Hooper	0	1*	1			2
						42							36

Ht 01: Etheridge, Sage, Askew, Sizmore	67.6	1 - 5
Ht 02: Young, Corradine, Spencer, Hooper	68.2	6 - 6
Ht 03: Bass, Broadbank, Leonard, Johns (f)	68.3	10 - 8
Ht 04: Handley, Sage, Hooper, Corradine (ef)	67.8	13 -11
Ht 05: Etheridge, Bass, Leonard, Broadbank	68.0	16 -14
Ht 06: Askew, Sage, Sizmore, Spencer	68.2	20 -16
Ht 07: Broadbank, Handley, Corradine, Johns (ef)	69.0	23 -19
Ht 08: Etheridge, Sizmore, Hooper, Young	68.5	25 -23
Ht 09: Leonard, Sage, Bass, Spencer	68.3	29 -25
Ht 10: Askew, Johns, Broadbank, Sizmore	68.4	32 -28
Ht 11: Handley, Etheridge, Johns, Young	67.8	35 -31
Ht 12: Askew, Sage, Leonard, Johns (f)	67.5	39 -33
Ht 13: Etheridge, Handley, Bass, Broadbank	67.8	42 -36

The Cheetahs had all been experiencing motor troubles over the previous weeks but Mick Handley had a new engine and the promoters appealed for anyone who knew of a Weslake engine available – they were in such demand.

Laurie Etheridge was the current New National League Riders Champion.

In the interval the crowd was entertained by the Mini-Mohican Junior Motor Cycle Stunt Team.

OXFORD CHEETAHS v CRAYFORD KESTRELS

Heat 1: Laurie Etheridge and Carl Askew

OXFORD CHEETAHS v CRAYFORD KESTRELS

Heat 1: Alan Sage, Roy Sizmore, Laurie Etheridge

Heat 2: Kevin Young, John Hooper, Gary Spencer, Mal Corradine

Heat 3: Brian Leonard

OXFORD CHEETAHS v CRAYFORD KESTRELS

Heat 3: Alan Johns (w), Mike Broadbank (yb) and Brian Leonard

Heat 4: Alan Sage, Mick Handley and John Hooper

OXFORD CHEETAHS v CRAYFORD KESTRELS

Heat 5: Mike Broadbank (yb), Phil Bass, Brian Leonard, Laurie Etheridge

Heat 6: Gary Spencer (yb), Carl Askew, Roy Sizmore, Alan Sage

Mick Handley

OXFORD CHEETAHS v MILDENHALL FEN TIGERS

1st July 1976

41-37

(National League)

Team Manager: Roger Jones   Team Manager (Tigers): Barry Klatt (?)

RIDERS INDIVIDUAL SCORE CHART													
OXFORD	**1**	**2**	**3**	**4**	**5**	**T**	**MILDENHALL**	**1**	**2**	**3**	**4**	**5**	**T**
1 Carl Askew	2	3	3	N		8	1 Bob Coles	3	1*	2	2*		14
2 Roy Sizmore	1*	2*	1	1		5	2 Rob Henry	F	0	T	N		0
3 Mick Handley	1*	2	R	F		3	3 Fred Mills	0	0	0	N		0
4 Jim Wells	3	3	3	1		10	4 Stan Stevens	2	3	0	N		5
5 Phil Bass	0	1	2*	2		5	5 Kevin Jolly						RR
6 Brian Leonard	2	2	1*	3		8	6 John Gibbons	0	1	1	2*	1	5
7 Kevin Young	1*	0	1			2	7 Alan Cowland	3	3	3	2	2	13
							8 Mick Bates	0	F				0
						41							37

Ht 01: Coles, Askew, Sizmore, Henry (f)	67.4	3 - 3
Ht 02: Cowland, Leonard, Young, Gibbons	68.0	6 - 6
Ht 03: Wells, Stevens, Coles, Bass	67.2	9 - 9
Ht 04: Cowland, Leonard, Handley, Mills	67.5	12 -12
Ht 05: Wells, Coles, Bass, Henry	66.5	16 -14
Ht 06: Askew, Sizmore, Gibbons, Mills	67.7	21 -15
Ht 07: Stevens, Handley, Leonard, Bates	68.0	24 -18
Ht 08: Cowland, Coles, Sizmore, Young	68.1	25 -23
Ht 09: Wells, Bass, Gibbons, Mills	67.5	30 -24
Ht 10: Askew, Cowland, Sizmore, Stevens	67.8	34 -26
Ht 11: Coles, Gibbons, Young, Handley (ret)	67.4	35 -31
Ht 12: Leonard, Cowland, Wells, Bates (f exc)	68.5	39 -33
Ht 13: Coles, Bass, Gibbons, Handley (f exc)	67.7	41 -37

OXFORD CHEETAHS v MILDENHALL FEN TIGERS

Bob Coles

Rob Henry

NB photos not from this match

ELLESMERE PORT GUNNERS v OXFORD CHEETAHS

6th July 1976

51-27

(National League)

Team Manager (Gunners): Joe Shaw   Team Manager: Roger Jones

RIDERS INDIVIDUAL SCORE CHART													
ELLESMERE PORT	1	2	3	4	5	T	OXFORD	1	2	3	4	5	T
1 John Jackson	3	3	3	3		12	1 Carl Askew	0	T	2	0		2
2 Gerald Smitherman	1	2*	2	1		6	2 Brian Leonard	2	2	0	0	T	4
3 Chris Turner	3	3	3	1*		10	3 Steve Holden	0	0	0	N	N	0
4 Robbie Gardner	3	3	3	2*		11	4 Phil Bass	1	0	T	O	N	1
5 Steve Finch	2*	0	2*	2		6	5 Kevin Young	E	1*	2	2	1	6
6 Louis Carr	0	2*	1			3	6 Roy Sizmore	2*	1	1	0	3	7
7 Duncan Meredith	1	1*	1			3	7 Jim Wells	3	1	3	0		7
						51							27

Ht 01: Jackson, Leonard, Smitherman, Askew   73.8   4 - 2

Ht 02: Wells, Sizmore, Meredith, Carr   76.4   5 - 7

Ht 03: Gardner, Finch, Bass, Young (ef)   76.0   10 - 8

Ht 04: Turner, Carr, Wells, Holden   76.8   15 - 9

Ht 05: Gardner, Leonard, Young, Finch   75.8   18 -12

Ht 06: Jackson, Smitherman, Sizmore, Holden   76.6   23 -13

Ht 07: Turner, Young, Carr, Bass   76.2   27 -15

Ht 08: Wells, Smitherman, Meredith, Leonard   77.2   30 -18

Ht 09: Gardner, Finch, Sizmore, Wells   76.6   35 -19

Ht 10: Jackson, Young, Smitherman, Leonard   76.6   39 -21

Ht 11: Turner, Askew, Meredith, Bass   77.2   43 -23

Ht 12: Jackson, Gardner, Young, Sizmore   76.6   48 -24

Ht 13: Sizmore, Finch, Turner, Askew   77.6   51 -27

OXFORD CHEETAHS v BERWICK BANDITS

8th July 1976

40-38

(National League KOC Quarter Final 1st Leg)

Team Manager: Roger Jones   Team Manager (Bandits): Kenny Taylor

OXFORD	1	2	3	4	5	T	BERWICK	1	2	3	4	5	6	7	T
1 Carl Askew	2	3	3	3		11	1 Mike Hiftle								RR
2 Kevin Young	1*	0	2*	0		3	2 Willie Templeton								RR
3 Mick Handley	2	2	3	1		8	3 Graham Jones	0	1*	1	1*	T			3
4 Brian Leonard	3	2	3	0		8	4 Robin Adlington	2	3	3	2	2			14
5 Phil Bass	1	0	N	N		1	5 Dave Gifford	3	0	1	1*	1*			6
6 Jim Wells	1	1*	0			2	6 Keith Williams	0	F	1	N	0	N	0	1
7 Roy Sizmore	3	3	E	1	0	7	7 Eddie Argall	2	3	2	N	2	2	3	14
							8 Wayne Brown								
						40									38

RIDERS INDIVIDUAL SCORE CHART

Ht 01: Gifford, Askew, Young, Williams	66.0	3 - 3
Ht 02: Sizmore, Argall, Wells, Williams (f exc)	67.4	7 - 5
Ht 03: Leonard, Adlington, Bass, Gifford (f rem)	67.0	11 - 7
Ht 04: Argall, Handley, Wells, Jones	66.3	14 -10
Ht 05: Adlington, Leonard, Williams, Bass	65.8	16 -14
Ht 06: Askew, Argall, Jones, Young	66.5	19 -17
Ht 07: Adlington, Handley, Gifford, Wells	67.2	21 -21
Ht 08: Sizmore, Young, Jones, Williams	67.5	26 -22
Ht 09: Leonard, Argall, Jones, Sizmore (ef)	66.9	29 -25
Ht 10: Askew, Adlington, Gifford, Young	66.5	32 -28
Ht 11: Handley, Argall, Sizmore, Williams	67.8	36 -30
Ht 12: Askew, Adlington, Gifford, Leonard	66.8	39 -33
Ht 13: Argall, Adlington, Handley, Sizmore	67.0	40 -38

MILDENHALL FEN TIGERS v OXFORD CHEETAHS

14th July 1976

48-30

(National League)

Team Manager (Tigers): Barry Klatt (?)   Team Manager: Roger Jones

RIDERS INDIVIDUAL SCORE CHART													
MILDENHALL	**1**	**2**	**3**	**4**	**5**	**T**	**OXFORD**	**1**	**2**	**3**	**4**	**5**	**T**
1 Bob Coles	3	3	3	3		12	1 Carl Askew	2	3	1	1*		9
2 Fred Mills	1	2*	3	0		6	2 Brian Leonard	0	1	T	2		3
3 Kevin Jolly	3	3	3	3		12	3 Mick Handley	1	1	2	1		5
4 John Gibbons	2	0	F	2*		4	4 Phil Bass	1	2	1*	1*		5
5 Stan Stevens	E	2	3	0		5	5 Kevin Young	3	0	F	2	0	5
6 Mick Bates	1	2*	1	2*		6	6 Roy Sizmore	0	0	T			0
7 Alan Cowland	3	X	0			3	7 Jim Wells	2	E	0	1*		3
						48							30

Ht 01: Coles, Askew, Mills, Leonard   60.6   4 - 2

Ht 02: Cowland, Wells, Bates, Sizmore   60.8   8 - 4

Ht 03: Young, Gibbons, Bass, Stevens (ef)   59.2   10 - 8

Ht 04: Jolly, Bates, Handley, Wells (ef)   61.2   15 - 9

Ht 05: Askew, Stevens, Leonard, Gibbons   60.0   17 -13

Ht 06: Coles, Mills, Handley, Sizmore   59.8   22 -14

Ht 07: Jolly, Bass, Bates, Young   59.2   26 -16

Ht 08: Mills, Bates, Askew, Wells, Cowland (ex tapes)   60.4   31 -17

Ht 09: Stevens, Handley, Wells, Gibbons (f exc),   60.6   34 -20

Young (f ns)

Ht 10: Coles, Young, Bass, Mills   58.6   37 -23

Ht 11: Jolly, Leonard, Askew, Cowland   59.0   40 -26

Ht 12: Coles, Gibbons, Handley, Young   59.2   45 -27

Ht 13: Jolly, Askew, Bass, Stevens   58.8   48 -30

ARTDEANS OF SWINDON BEST PAIRS CHAMPIONSHIP

15th July 1976

(at Oxford)

RIDERS	1	2	3	4	5	6	Pts	Tpts
01 Martin Yeates	3	3	3	3	3	3	18	25
02 Carl Askew	1	2	0	2	1	1	7	
03. Phil Bass	2	1	1	1	2	1	8	13
04. Jim Wells	0	2	0	0	3	0	5	
05. Brian Clark	2	3	1	3	1	3	13	20
06. Kevin Young	1	0	2	2	2	0	7	
07. Rob Hollingworth	3	3	2	3	0	3	14	25
08. Roy Sizmore	0	2	3	2	2	2	11	
09. Alan Sage	2	0	3	2	2	2	11	19
10. Brian Leonard	3	1	0	3	0	1	8	
11. Mick Handley	0	1	1	0	n	n	2	9
12. Bob Garrad	1	3	e	1	1	1	7	
13. Barney Kennett	1	2	2	1	3	3	12	15
14 Steve Holden	0	f	1	0	0	2	3	
Res: Keith Pilcher	0						0	
Res: John Williams	0						0	

Martin Yeates
[*NB photo from a different occasion*]

ARTDEANS OF SWINDON BEST PAIRS CHAMPIONSHIP

15th July 1976

Ht 01: Yeates, Bass, Askew, Wells	66.6
Ht 02: Hollingworth, Clark, Young, Sizmore	66.9
Ht 03: Leonard, Sage, Garrad, Handley	67.1
Ht 04: Yeates, Askew, Kennett, Holden	65.6
Ht 05: Clark, Wells, Bass, Young	67.1
Ht 06: Hollingworth, Sizmore, Leonard, Sage	66.5
Ht 07: Garrad, Kennett, Handley, Holden (f exc)	67.4
Ht 08: Yeates, Young, Clark, Askew	66.2
Ht 09: Sizmore, Hollingworth, Bass, Wells	67.0
Ht 10: Sage, Kennett, Holden, Leonard	67.5
Ht 11: Yeates, Askew, Handley, Garrad (ef)	66.8
Ht 12: Leonard, Sage, Bass, Wells	67.6
Ht 13: Clark, Young, Garrad, Handley	66.0
Ht 14: Hollingworth, Sizmore, Kennett, Holden	67.0
Ht 15: Yeates, Sage, Askew, Leonard	65.7
Ht 16: Wells, Bass, Garrad, Pilcher	68.0
Ht 17: Kennett, Young, Clark, Holden	67.3
Ht 18: Yeates, Sizmore, Askew, Hollingworth	66.2
Ht 19: Kennett, Holden, Bass, Wells	68.2
Ht 20: Clark, Sage, Leonard, Young	67.5
Ht 21: Hollingworth, Sizmore, Garrad, Williams	67.4

Run off for 1st place: Yeates, Hollingworth, Askew, Sizmore

BERWICK BANDITS v OXFORD CHEETAHS

17th July 1976

48-30

Agg: Berwick 86 - 70 Oxford

(National League KOC Quarter Final 2nd Leg)

Team Manager (Bandits): Kenny Taylor   Team Manager: Roger Jones

RIDERS INDIVIDUAL SCORE CHART													
BERWICK	**1**	**2**	**3**	**4**	**5**	**T**	**OXFORD**	**1**	**2**	**3**	**4**	**5**	**T**
1 Mike Hiftle	2*	3	F	3	2*	10	1 Roy Sizmore	0	0	N	1		1
2 Willie Templeton						RR	2 Brian Leonard	1	1	2	2		6
3 Graham Jones	3	R	R	N	N	3	3 Mick Handley	2	0	T	0		2
4 Robin Adlington	3	2*	2*	3		10	4 Phil Bass	2	2	2*	2	3	11
5 Dave Gifford	X	1	3	3	2	9	5 Kevin Young	0	3	1	1*	1	6
6 Keith Williams	1	1	1	0	0	3	6 Ian Darling (G)	0	T	0			0
7 Eddie Argall	3	3	1	3	3	13	7 Jim Wells	2	0	1*	1*		4
8 Peter Waite													
						48							30

Ht 01: Argall, Hiftle, Leonard, Sizmore, Gifford (ex tapes)   73.4   5 - 1

Ht 02: Argall, Wells, Williams, Darling   73.8   9 - 3

Ht 03: Adlington, Bass, Gifford, Young   76.0   13 - 5

Ht 04: Jones, Handley, Williams, Wells   76.2   17 - 7

Ht 05: Gifford, Adlington, Leonard, Sizmore   76.6   22 - 8

Ht 06: Hiftle, Bass, Argall, Handley   75.4   26 -10

Ht 07: Young, Bass, Williams, Jones (ret)   75.0   27 -15

Ht 08: Argall, Leonard, Wells, Hiftle (f)   74.8   30 -18

Ht 09: Gifford, Adlington, Young, Darling   76.2   35 -19

Ht 10: Hiftle, Bass, Young, Jones (ret)   74.8   38 -22

Ht 11: Argall, Leonard, Wells, Williams   76.6   41 -25

Ht 12: Adlington, Hiftle, Young, Handley   77.0   46 -26

Ht 13: Bass, Gifford, Sizmore, Williams   76.0   48 -30

OXFORD CHEETAHS v PAISLEY LIONS

22nd July 1976

56-22

(National League)

Team Manager: Roger Jones   Team Manager (Lions): Neil MacFarlane

OXFORD	1	2	3	4	5	T	PAISLEY	1	2	3	4	5	T
						RIDERS INDIVIDUAL SCORE CHART							
1 Carl Askew	3	2*	3	2*		10	1 Mike Fishwick	0	2	0	1	1*	4
2 Brian Leonard	2*	3	3	2*		10	2 Alan Bridgett	1	0	2	0		3
3 Mick Handley	2*	2	3	3		10	3 Stuart Mountford	1	1	1	1		4
4 Kevin Young	3	1	3	3		10	4 Colin Farqharson	2	3	0	1	2	8
5 Steve Holden	F	3	2*	F		5	5 Mike Fullerton	1*	1	0	0		2
6 Jim Wells	3	3	0			6	6 Mick Sheldrick	0	0	T			0
7 Roy Sizmore	2*	1	2*			5	7 Malcolm Chambers	1	0	T			1
						56							22

Ht 01: Askew, Leonard, Bridgett, Fishwick	67.0	5 - 1
Ht 02: Wells, Sizmore, Chambers, Sheldrick	66.9	10 - 2
Ht 03: Young, Farquharson, Fullerton, Holden (f exc)	65.9	13 - 5
Ht 04: Wells, Handley, Mountford, Chambers	67.1	18 - 6
Ht 05: Holden, Fishwick, Young, Bridgett	68.8	22 - 8
Ht 06: Leonard, Askew, Mountford, Sheldrick	66.6	27 - 9
Ht 07: Farquharson, Handley, Fullerton, Wells	67.0	29 -13
Ht 08: Leonard, Bridgett, Sizmore, Fishwick (f rem)	66.8	33 -15
Ht 09: Young, Holden, Mountford, Farquharson	67.6	38 -16
Ht 10: Askew, Leonard, Farquharson, Fullerton	67.5	43 -17
Ht 11: Handley, Sizmore, Fishwick, Bridgett	67.7	48 -18
Ht 12: Young, Askew, Mountford, Fullerton	67.6	53 -19
Ht 13: Handley, Farquharson, Fishwick, Holden (f)	67.4	56 -22

WEYMOUTH WIZARDS v OXFORD CHEETAHS

27th July 1976

41-36

(National League)

Team Manager (Wizards): Joe Bargery   Team Manager: Roger Jones

RIDERS INDIVIDUAL SCORE CHART													
WEYMOUTH	**1**	**2**	**3**	**4**	**5**	**T**	**OXFORD**	**1**	**2**	**3**	**4**	**5**	**T**
1 Martin Yeates	3	3	3	3		12	1 Carl Askew	2	2*	2	X		6
2 Roger Stratton	R	0	T	T		0	2 Brian Leonard	1*	3	2	0		6
3 Chris Robins	2	2	2*	1	3	10	3 Mick Handley	1	1*	2	2		6
4 Gary May	0	R	N	N		0	4 Phil Bass	1*	1	1	1		4
5 Vic Harding	3	F	F	3	2*	8	5 Kevin Young	2	3	X	0		5
6 Jack Walker	1	0	0			1	6 Roy Sizmore	2	2	1*	0		5
7 Danny Kennedy	3	3	0	3	1	10	7 Jim Wells	0	3	1*			4
						41							36

Ht 01: Yeates, Askew, Leonard, Stratton (ret)   72.4   3 - 3

Ht 02: Kennedy, Sizmore, Walker, Wells   73.5   7 - 5

Ht 03: Harding, Young, Bass, May   72.5   10 - 8

Ht 04: Wells, Robins, Handley, Walker   75.0   12 -12

Ht 05: Leonard, Askew, May (ret), Harding (f exc)   73.9   12 -17

Ht 06: Yeates, Sizmore, Handley, Stratton   71.6   15 -20

Ht 07: Young, Robins, Bass, Walker   72.3   17 -24

Ht 08: Kennedy, Leonard, Wells, Harding (f)   74.4   20 -27

Ht 09: Harding, Handley, Sizmore, Kennedy   74.5   23 -30

Ht 10: Yeates, Robins, Bass, Sizmore, Young (exc)   72.5   28 -31

Ht 11: Kennedy, Askew, Robins, Leonard   73.8   32 -33

Ht 12: Yeates, Handley, Kennedy, Young   72.0   36 -35

Ht 13: Robins, Harding, Bass, Askew (ex boring)   73.0   41 -36

OXFORD CHEETAHS v PETERBOROUGH PANTHERS

29th July 1976

44-34

(National League)

Team Manager: Roger Jones   Team Manager (Panthers): Ron Orchard

RIDERS INDIVIDUAL SCORE CHART													
OXFORD	**1**	**2**	**3**	**4**	**5**	**T**	**PETERBOROUGH**	**1**	**2**	**3**	**4**	**5**	**T**
1 Carl Askew	3	2	0	2		7	1 Tony Featherstone	2	1	F	N		3
2 Steve Holden	1	0	N	N		1	2 Steve Taylor	F	0	N	T		0
3 Mick Handley	3	1	3	E		7	3 Roy Carter	0	T	1	0		1
4 Kevin Young	0	3	3	1*		7	4 Ken Matthews	3	0	0	3	2*	8
5 Phil Bass	1	2*	2*	1		6	5 Brian Clark	2*	3	2	3*	3	12
6 Jim Wells	3	2*	1	2*		11	6 Nigel Couzens	2	1	0	T	3	6
7 Roy Sizmore	0	2*	1	2*		5	7 Kevin Hawkins	1	1	1	1		4
						44							34

Ht 01: Askew, Featherstone, Holden (f rem), Taylor (f exc)   68.4   4 - 2

Ht 02: Wells, Couzens, Hawkins, Sizmore   66.5   7 - 5

Ht 03: Matthews, Clark, Bass, Young   67.8   8 -10

Ht 04: Handley, Wells, Hawkins, Carter   67.4   13 -11

Ht 05: Young, Bass, Featherstone, Taylor   67.2   18 -12

Ht 06: Clark, Askew, Couzens, Holden   66.6   20 -16

Ht 07: Wells, Clark, Handley, Matthews   66.8   24 -18

Ht 08: Wells, Sizmore, Hawkins, Couzens   67.5   29 -19

Ht 09: Young, Bass, Carter, Matthews   67.4   34 -20

Ht 10: Matthews, Clark, Sizmore, Askew   67.7   35 -25

Ht 11: Handley, Sizmore, Hawkins, Featherstone (f)   68.4   40 -26

Ht 12: Clark, Askew, Young, Carter   66.7   43 -29

Ht 13: Couzens, Matthews, Bass, Handley (ef)   67.5   44 -34

PAISLEY LIONS v OXFORD CHEETAHS

31st July 1976

48-30

(National League)

Team Manager (Lions): Neil MacFarlane   Team Manager: Roger Jones

RIDERS INDIVIDUAL SCORE CHART													
PAISLEY	1	2	3	4	5	T	OXFORD	1	2	3	4	5	T
1 Stuart Mountford	3	3	2	3		11	1 Carl Askew	2	1	3	2	2*	10
2 Alan Bridgett	0	2*	X	1*		3	2 Brian Leonard	1*	0	2*	1*		4
3 Mike Fishwick	3	3	3	0		9	3 Mick Handley	1	1	0	1		3
4 Colin Farquharson	2*	3	3	2*		10	4 Phil Bass	1	2	2	3	3	11
5 Mike Fullerton	3	2*	1	1		7	5 Kevin Young	0	0	X	0		0
6 Mick Sheldrick	3	2*	1	1		7	6 Jim Wells	0	0	T			0
7 Colin Caffrey	1	0	0			1	7 Roy Sizmore	2	0	T	0		2
						48							30

Ht 01: Mountford, Askew, Leonard, Bridgett   78.0   3 - 3

Ht 02: Sheldrick, Sizmore, Caffrey, Wells   81.6   7 - 5

Ht 03: Fullerton, Farquharson, Bass, Young   78.0   12 - 6

Ht 04: Fishwick, Sheldrick, Handley, Sizmore   78.0   17 - 7

Ht 05: Farquharson, Fullerton, Askew, Leonard   76.6   22 - 8

Ht 06: Mountford, Bridgett, Handley, Wells   78.2   27 - 9

Ht 07: Fishwick, Bass, Sheldrick, Young   78.0   31 -11

Ht 08: Askew, Leonard, Sheldrick, Caffrey,   78.4   32 -16

                Bridgett(ex tapes)

Ht 09: Farquharson, Bass, Fullerton, Handlcy   76.8   36 -18

Ht 10: Bass, Mountford, Bridgett, Sizmore,   78.2   39 -21

              Young (ex tapes)

Ht 11: Fishwick, Askew, Leonard, Caffrey   78.0   42 -24

Ht 12: Mountford, Farquharson, Handley, Young   79.0   47 -25

Ht 13: Bass, Askew, Fullerton, Fishwick   79.6   48 -30

171

OXFORD CHEETAHS v EASTBOURNE EAGLES

5th August 1976

53-25

(National League)

Team Manager: Roger Jones   Team Manager (Eagles): Arthur Nutley

RIDERS INDIVIDUAL SCORE CHART														
OXFORD	1	2	3	4	5	T	**EASTBOURNE**	1	2	3	4	5	6	T
1 Carl Askew	E	3	3	2		8	1 Eric Dugard	2*	2	0	T	1		5
2 Brian Leonard	1	2*	1	2*		6	2 Steve Weatherley							RR
3 Mick Handley	3	3	1	3		10	3 Colin Richardson	3	F	1	2	1	1	8
4 Kevin Young	3	F	N	0		3	4 Pete Jarman	E	R	T	N			0
5 Phil Bass	2*	3	2*	2*		9	5 Roger Abel	1	1	1	2	3		8
6 Jim Wells	3	2*	2*	3		10	6 Ian Fletcher	2	1*	0	0	0		3
7 Roy Sizmore	1	3	3			7	7 Ian Gledhill	0	1	T				1
							8 Mike Pither	0	0					0
						53								25

Ht 01: Richardson, Dugard, Leonard, Askew (ef)	67.6	1 - 5
Ht 02: Wells, Fletcher, Sizmore, Gledhill	68.2	5 - 7
Ht 03: Young, Bass, Abel, Jarman (ef)	67.7	10 - 8
Ht 04: Handley, Wells, Gledhill, Richardson (f exc)	68.4	15 - 9
Ht 05: Bass, Dugard, Fletcher, Young (f exc)	68.3	18 -12
Ht 06: Askew, Leonard, Richardson, Fletcher	68.2	23 -13
Ht 07: Handley, Wells, Abel, Jarman (ret)	68.6	28 -14
Ht 08: Sizmore, Richardson, Leonard, Pither	68.5	32 -16
Ht 09: Wells, Bass, Richardson, Fletcher	69.0	37 -17
Ht 10: Askew, Leonard, Abel, Dugard	68.2	42 -18
Ht 11: Sizmore, Abel, Handley, Pither	68.4	46 -20
Ht 12: Abel, Askew, Richardson, Young	68.6	48 -20
Ht 13: Handley, Bass, Dugard, Fletcher	69.1	53 -25

OXFORD CHEETAHS v EASTBOURNE EAGLES
5th August 1976

PROGRAMME NOTES FROM THE PROMOTERS

May I, on behalf of the riders, congratulate Mr George Squires and his right hand man, Bill Spicer, on the marvellous job they are doing in preparing the track for our Thursday evening's entertainment. Smiler Mick, probably one of the most critical of riders, said that it was getting better week by week, and for Smiler to say that is praise indeed.

Besides team strengthening, stadium improvements still remain at the forefront of our minds and we would hope that these will be put in hand during the next few weeks.

It's good to see our second half juniors progressing so well, improvement is what you ask and look for and in the case of our second half lads, the improvement is there for everyone to see. I, for one, would not be at all surprised to see at least one of them "blooded" in the team in the very near future.

The team, although they are still looking for their first away win, will continue to provide value for money entertainment during visit to away tracks, so much so in fact that no less than five of our riders were invited back to appear in an open individual event at Weymouth speedway. This would, I think, qualify as some sort of record. A fortnight ago, super sportswriter Tom Goodway surprised everyone in the the bar by challenging any other sports journalist to a speedway race. I believe that the challenge has been accepted by sports photographer, Keith Lawson, but I will keep you informed if this is confirmed.

Notes: being in the New National League meant away matches were much further to travel and fans could not get easily to matches and vice versa, which affected gate figures. And Tom either got cold feet or sobered up (only kidding) as the race never happened.

OXFORD CHEETAHS v CANTERBURY CRUSADERS

12th August 1976

41-37

(National League)

Team Manager: Roger Jones   Team Manager (Crusaders):

RIDERS INDIVIDUAL SCORE CHART													
OXFORD	**1**	**2**	**3**	**4**	**5**	**T**	**CANTERBURY**	**1**	**2**	**3**	**4**	**5**	**T**
1 Carl Askew	3	2*	2	N		7	1 Les Rumsey	2	3	2	0		7
2 Brian Leonard	1	3	1*	0		5	2 Reg Luckhurst	0	0	0	N		0
3 Mick Handley	1*	1	3	1*		6	3 Barney Kennett	0	1	0	T		1
4 Kevin Young	1*	2	1	2		6	4 Steve Koppe	3	2*	1	3		9
5 Phil Bass	2	1*	3	2		8	5 Graham Banks	0	3	3	1	3	10
6 Jim Wells	3	2	0	0		5	6 Terry Casserly	0	F	N			0
7 Roy Sizmore	1	2	1			4	7 Graham Clifton	2	3	3	2	F	10
						41							37

Ht 01: Askew, Rumsey, Leonard, Luckhurst	66.2	4 - 2
Ht 02: Wells, Clifton, Sizmore, Casserly	66.9	8 - 4
Ht 03: Koppe, Bass, Young, Banks	66.6	11 - 7
Ht 04: Clifton, Wells, Handley, Kennett	66.3	14 -10
Ht 05: Rumsey, Young, Bass, Luckhurst	66.8	17 -13
Ht 06: Leonard, Askew, Kennett, Casserly (f exc)	67.1	22 -14
Ht 07: Banks, Koppe, Handley, Wells	66.3	23 -19
Ht 08: Clifton, Sizmore, Leonard, Luckhurst	66.8	26 -22
Ht 09: Bass, Clifton, Young, Kennett	66.8	30 -24
Ht 10: Banks, Askew, Koppe, Leonard	66.8	32 -28
Ht 11: Handley, Rumsey, Sizmore, Clifton (f exc)	66.0	36 -30
Ht 12: Koppe, Young, Banks, Wells	67.1	38 -34
Ht 13: Banks, Bass, Handley, Rumsey	66.9	41- 37

Reg Luckhurst (1975)

OXFORD CHEETAHS v CANTERBURY CRUSADERS

As no photos from this meeting have survived, I have taken these from an 1977 archive.

Barney Kennett

Graham Banks

Graham Clifton

Steve Koppe

STOKE POTTERS v OXFORD CHEETAHS

14th August 1976

45-33

(National League)

Team Manager (Potters): Chris Harrison   Team Manager: Roger Jones

STOKE	1	2	3	4	5	T	OXFORD	1	2	3	4	5	T
1 Les Collins	0	1	3	3	3	10	1 Carl Askew	2	2	R	T		4
2 Jim Brett	3	1	0	2	1	7	2 Brian Leonard	1*	0	1	2	1*	5
3 Jack Millen	3	2	3	3	3	14	3 Jim Wells	0	T	2	2		4
4 Ricky Day						RR	4 Phil Bass	3	3	3	2	2	13
5 Steve McDermott	0	N	1	0		1	5 Kevin Young	2*	2	0	0	N	4
6 Mick Newton	3	2*	3	1*		9	6 Roy Sizmore	1	1*	N			2
7 Tim Nunan	2*	0	1			3	7 Colin Meredith	0	1	T	0	0	1
8 Andy Reid	1					1							
						45							33

Ht 01: Brett, Askew, Leonard, Collins   69.9   3 - 3

Ht 02: Newton, Nunan, Sizmore, Meredith   69.4   8 - 4

Ht 03: Bass, Young, Brett, McDermott   69.8   9 - 9

Ht 04: Millen, Newton, Meredith, Wells   69.7   14 -10

Ht 05: Newton, Askew, Collins, Leonard   70.2   18 -12

Ht 06: Collins, Young, Sizmore, Brett   68.8   21 -15

Ht 07: Bass, Millen, Newton, Young   69.7   24 -18

Ht 08: Bass, Brett, Leonard, Nunan   70.1   26 -22

Ht 09: Millen, Wells, McDermott, Meredith   69.6   30 -24

Ht 10: Collins, Bass, Brett, Young   69.8   34 -26

Ht 11: Millen, Leonard, Nunan, Askew (ret)   70.1   38 -28

Ht 12: Collins, Wells, Reid, Meredith   69.7   42 -30

Ht 13: Millen, Bass, Leonard, McDermott   70.6   45 -33

The arrival of Colin Meredith as a Cheetah

OXFORD CHEETAHS v BOSTON BARRACUDAS

19ᵗʰ August 1976

57-21

(National League)

Team Manager: Roger Jones   Team Manager (Barracudas):

RIDERS INDIVIDUAL SCORE CHART														
OXFORD	**1**	**2**	**3**	**4**	**5**	**T**	**BOSTON**	**1**	**2**	**3**	**4**	**5**	**6**	**T**
1 Carl Askew	3	3	2*	2*		10	1 Billy Burton							RR
2 Brian Leonard	1	2*	3	3		9	2 Chris Emery	0	2	0	1			3
3 Mick Handley	1	N	3	2*		6	3 Martin Yeates(G)	2	0	1	3	0	1	7
4 Kevin Young	N	3	1*	3		7	4 Trevor Whiting	0	2	0	1			3
5 Phil Bass	2*	1	2	3		8	5 Stuart Cope	1	E	F	1	N		2
6 Jim Wells	1	3	3			7	6 Ron Cooper	F	0	N	0			0
7 Roy Sizmore	3	3	1	1	2*	10	7 Steve Clarke	2	2	2	0	0		6
							8 Dave Allen							
					57									21

Ht 01: Askew, Yeates, Leonard, Emery   **NL TR**   65.2   4 - 2

Ht 02: Sizmore, Clarke, Wells, Cooper (f)   67.3   8 - 4

Ht 03: Sizmore, Bass, Cope, Whiting   67.4   13 - 5

Ht 04: Wells, Clarke, Handley, Yeates   65.8   17 - 7

Ht 05: Young, Emery, Bass, Cope (ef)   67.2   21 - 9

Ht 06: Askew, Leonard, Yeates, Cooper   67.0   26 -10

Ht 07: Wells, Whiting, Sizmore, Cope (f)   66.9   30 -12

Ht 08: Leonard, Clarke, Sizmore, Emery   67.1   34 -14

Ht 09: Yeates, Bass, Young, Clarke   66.0   37 -17

Ht 10: Leonard, Askew, Cope, Whiting   68.1   42 -18

Ht 11: Handley, Sizmore, Emery, Yeates   67.2   47 -19

Ht 12: Young, Askew, Yeates, Clarke   67.5   52 -20

Ht 13: Bass, Handley, Whiting, Cooper   67.6   57 -21

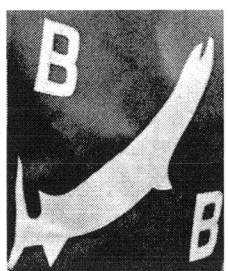

OXFORD CHEETAHS v WEYMOUTH WIZARDS

26th August 1976

51-27

(National League)

Team Manager: Roger Jones   Team Manager (Wizards):Joe Bargery

RIDERS INDIVIDUAL SCORE CHART													
OXFORD	**1**	**2**	**3**	**4**	**5**	**T**	**WEYMOUTH**	**1**	**2**	**3**	**4**	**5**	**T**
1 Carl Askew	1*	2*	1	2*		6	1 Martin Yeates	3	3	3	E	T	9
2 Brian Leonard	2	3	2	3		10	2 Danny Kennedy	0	1	0	T	1	2
3 Mick Handley	2	1	2*	2*		7	3 Jack Walker	1	0	N	N	0	1
4 Kevin Young	2*	2	2*	3		9	4 Gerald Purkiss	1	0	0	T		1
5 Jim Wells	3	F	3	3		9	5 Vic Harding	0	2	2	1	1	6
6 Colin Meredith	E	E	3			3	6 Garry May	1*	1	0			2
7 Roy Sizmore	3	1*	3			7	7 Billy Spiers	2	3	T	1	0	6
						51							27

Ht 01: Yeates, Leonard, Askew, Kennedy   66.6   3 - 3

Ht 02: Sizmore, Spiers, May, Meredith (ef)   67.8   6 - 6

Ht 03: Wells, Young, Purkiss, Harding   67.2   11 - 7

Ht 04: Spiers, Handley, Walker, Meredith (ef)   67.0   13 -11

Ht 05: Yeates, Young, Kennedy, Wells (f exc)   65.9   15 -15

Ht 06: Leonard, Askew, May, Walker   67.1   20 -16

Ht 07: Meredith, Harding, Handley, Purkiss   67.4   24 -18

Ht 08: Yeates, Leonard, Sizmore, Kennedy   66.3   27 -21

Ht 09: Wells, Young, Spiers, May   67.3   32 -22

Ht 10: Leonard, Harding, Askew, Purkiss   67.0   36 -24

Ht 11: Sizmore, Handley, Harding, Yeates (ef)   67.9   41 -25

Ht 12: Young, Askew, Harding, Spiers   67.6   46 - 26

Ht 13: Wells, Handley, Kennedy, Walker   68.5   51 -27

Harry Bastable asked me to organise a stadium collection for Colin Meredith, who needed funds to kit himself properly. Steve Windle, the Cheetahs' mascot and I carried a blanket round the stands and the fans were incredibly generous. The Supporters Club took the blanket away to count the money but I cannot recall how much was raised.

OXFORD v COVENTRY v SWINDON v WHITE CITY
2nd September 1976
(Inter League Four Team Tournament)

RIDERS INDIVIDUAL SCORE CHART

OXFORD	1	2	3	4	T	WHITE CITY	1	2	3	4	T
1 Phil Bass	2	0	1	1	4	1 Gordon Kennett	3	3	3	3	12
2 Mick Handley	E	0	N	0	0	2 Paul Gachet	2	3	1	1	7
3 Kevin Young	0	2	0	1	3	3 Dag Lovaas	3	3	3	1	10
4 Carl Askew	3	0	1	0	4	4 Trevor Geer	3	1	2	3	9
5 Brian Leonard	1				1						
					12						38

SWINDON	1	2	3	4	T	COVENTRY	1	2	3	4	T
1 Bob Kilby	F	N	N	N	0	1 Mitch Shirra	2	3	3	2	10
2 Martin Ashby	1	2	2	3	8	2 John Harrhy	0	0	2	2	4
3 Geoff Bouchard	1	2	2	2	7	3 Ole Olsen	2	N	3	3	8
4 David Ashby	1	2	0	2	5	4 Alan Molyneux	F	N	N	N	0
5 Colin Meredith(G)	0	1	0		1	5 Roy Sizmore(G)	1	1	1	0	3
6 Brian Leonard(G)	0				0	6 Jim Wells (G)	0				0
					21						25

Ht 01: Askew, Gachet, Sizmore, Meredith, Molyneux (f ns),

                Kilby (f ns)   66.8

Ht 02: Kennett, Olsen, M.Ashby, Young (NL TR)   64.2

Ht 03: Lovaas, Shirra, D.Ashby, Handley (ef)   66.5

Ht 04: Geer, Bass, Bouchard, Harrhy   65.6

Ht 05: Shirra, M.Ashby, Geer, Askew   65.4

Ht 06: Lovaas, Young, Meredith, Harrhy   65.8

Ht 07: Kennett, Bouchard, Sizmore, Handley   64.4

Ht 08: Gachet, D.Ashby, Sizmore, Bass   66.6

Ht 09: Kennett, Harrhy, Askew, D.Ashby   64.8

Ht 10: Shirra, Bouchard, Gachet, Young   65.9

Ht 11: Olsen, Geer, Leonard, Meredith   65.5

Ht 12: Lovaas, M.Ashby, Bass, Sizmore   66.2

Ht 13: Geer, D.Ashby, Young, Wells   66.0

Ht 14: Olsen, Bouchard, Lovaas, Askew   65.2

Ht 15: M.Ashby, Harrhy, Gachet, Handley   65.8

Ht 16: Kennett, Shirra, Bass, Leonard   65.1

OXFORD v COVENTRY v SWINDON v WHITE CITY

Ole Olsen

Dag Lovaas

Gordon Kennett

Martin Ashby

Bob Kilby

OXFORD CHEETAHS v BERWICK BANDITS

9th September 1976

56-22

(National League)

Team Manager: Roger Jones   Team Manager (Bandits): Kenny Taylor

RIDERS INDIVIDUAL SCORE CHART													
OXFORD	1	2	3	4	5	T	BERWICK	1	2	3	4	5	T
1 Carl Askew	2*	3	3	3		11	1 Mike Hiftle	E	2	0	0	0	2
2 Brian Leonard	3	2*	3	2*		10	2 Willie Templeton	1	1*	0	N		2
3 Mick Handley	0	2*	2*	1		5	3 Graham Jones	2	1	2	2	2	9
4 Jim Wells	3	0	1	1		5	4 Robin Adlington	1	E	E	T		1
5 Phil Bass	2*	3	3	3		11	5 Dave Gifford	0	1	1	0		2
6 Kevin Young	1	3	3			7	6 Wayne Brown	0	0	T			0
7 Roy Sizmore	3	1	3			7	7 Eddie Argall	2	1*	2	1		6
						56							22

Ht 01: Leonard, Askew, Templeton, Hiftle (ef)   67.6   5 - 1

Ht 02: Sizmore, Argall, Young, Brown   69.0   9 - 3

Ht 03: Wells, Bass, Adlington, Gifford   67.6   14 - 4

Ht 04: Young, Jones, Argall, Handley   68.4   17 - 7

Ht 05: Bass, Hiftle, Templeton, Wells   68.2   20 -10

Ht 06: Askew, Leonard, Jones, Brown   68.0   25 -11

Ht 07: Young, Handley, Gifford, Adlington (ef)   68.7   30 -12

Ht 08: Leonard, Argall, Sizmore, Templeton   67.2   34 -14

Ht 09: Bass, Jones, Wells, Hiftle   66.8   38 -16

Ht 10: Askew, Leonard, Gifford, Adlington (ef)   69.0   43 -17

Ht 11: Sizmore, Handley, Argall, Hiftle   68.8   48 -18

Ht 12: Askew, Jones, Wells, Gifford   67.4   52 -20

Ht 13: Bass, Jones, Handley, Hiftle   67.3   56 -22

A cold, wet and windy night but 3 Cheetahs with paid maximums.

"Go to Jail, go directly to Jail....."

PETERBOROUGH PANTHERS v OXFORD CHEETAHS

10th September 1976

40-0

(National League)

Team Manager (Panthers): Ron Orchard   Team Manager: Roger Jones

RIDERS INDIVIDUAL SCORE CHART													
PETERBOROUGH	**1**	**2**	**3**	**4**	**5**	**T**	**OXFORD**	**1**	**2**	**3**	**4**	**5**	**T**
1 Tony Featherstone	2*	3				5	1 Carl Askew						
2 Roy Carter	3	2*	2*			7	2 Brian Leonard						
3 Ken Matthews	3	2*				5	3 Mick Handley						
4 Steve Taylor	2*	2*				4	4 Jim Wells						
5 Brian Clark	3	3				6	5 Phil Bass						
6 Kevin Hawkins	2*	2*	3			7	6 Roy Sizmore						
7 Nigel Couzens	3	3				6	7 Kevin Young						
						40							0

Ht 01: Carter, Featherstone, Askew (ns), Leonard (ns)   76.6

Ht 02: Couzens, Hawkins, Sizmore (ns), Young (ns)   83.4

Ht 03: Clark, Taylor, Wells (ns), Bass (ns)   70.8

t 04: Matthews, Hawkins, Handley (ns), Young (ns)   73.4

Ht 05: Clark, Taylor, Askew (ns), Leonard (ns)   72.0

Ht 06: Featherstone, Carter, Handley (ns), Sizmore (ns)   75.0

Ht 07: Hawkins, Matthews, Wells (ns), Bass (ns)   74.8

Ht 08: Couzens, Carter, Leonard (ns), Young (ns)   79.0

Ht 09:

Ht 10:

Ht 11:

Ht 12:

Ht 13:

The Oxford team refused to race on a wet track but the referee allowed the Panthers to ride uncontested and the result was allowed to stand plus the Cheetahs were fined. Carl Askew, as the Captain, had to report to the referee that they would not ride, although he personally was prepared to give it go but stood united with a team decision.

The same night, the match between Workington and Teeside was postponed due to rain!

OXFORD CHEETAHS v SCUNTHORPE SAINTS

16th September 1976

41-37

(National League)

Team Manager: Roger Jones   Team Manager (Saints): Les Allum

RIDERS INDIVIDUAL SCORE CHART													
OXFORD	1	2	3	4	5	T	SCUNTHORPE	1	2	3	4	5	T
1 Carl Askew	2*	1	0	2		5	1 Keith Evans	1	3	2	3	1*	10
2 Brian Leonard	3	3	1	2		9	2 Colin Cook	0	0	0	T		0
3 Kevin Young	2	0	0	0		2	3 Sid Sheldrick	0	N	O	T		0
4 Jim Wells	2*	1*	1	0		4	4 Phil Kynman	1	3	3	3	2	12
5 Phil Bass	3	2	3	3		11	5 Andy Hines	0	1	1	2*	1	5
6 Pip Lamb	1*	1*	2			4	6 Ray Watkins	0	0	T			0
7 Roy Sizmore	2	3	1			6	7 Tony Boyle	3	3	2	2		10
						41							37

Ht 01: Leonard, Askew, Evans, Cook	**NL TR** 64.6		5 - 1
Ht 02: Boyle, Sizmore, Lamb, Watkins	67.6		8 - 4
Ht 03: Bass, Wells, Kynman, Hines	67.0		13 - 5
Ht 04: Boyle, Young, Lamb, Sheldrick	66.2		16 - 8
Ht 05: Evans, Bass, Wells, Cook (f rem)	66.6		19 -11
Ht 06: Leonard, Boyle, Askew, Watkins	65.6		23 -13
Ht 07: Kynman, Lamb, Hines, Young	66.3		25 -17
Ht 08: Sizmore, Boyle, Leonard, Cook	66.8		29 -19
Ht 09: Bass, Evans, Wells, Sheldrick	66.4		33 -21
Ht 10: Kynman, Leonard, Hines, Askew	66.5		35 25
Ht 11: Evans, Hines, Sizmore, Young	67.5		36 -30
Ht 12: Kynman, Askew, Hines, Wells	66.5		38 -34
Ht 13: Bass, Kynman, Evans, Young	65.6		41 -37

The programme carried an "advert" from Mick Handley – selling a 1975 standard Jawa for £375. Mick had fallen off scaffolding in his day job as bricklayer, so Kevin Young moved up to #3 and Pip Lamb filled the #6 berth.

As Cheetahs with the most bonus points, Jim Wells and Pip Lamb won a bottle of champagne that I and John Hall (fellow photographer) had sponsored.

OXFORD CHEETAHS v ELLESMERE PORT GUNNERS

23rd September 1976

47-30

(National League)

Team Manager (Gunners): Joe Shaw   Team Manager: Roger Jones

RIDERS INDIVIDUAL SCORE CHART														
OXFORD	1	2	3	4	5	T	ELLESMERE	1	2	3	4	5	6	T
1 Carl Askew	2*	3	3	3		11	1 John Jackson	F	2	3	2	1	3	11
2 Mick Handley	3	2*	F	1		6	2 Gerald Smitherman	F	T	3	3	0	0	6
3 Brian Leonard	3	3	3	1*		10	3 Chris Turner							RR
4 Jim Wells	1	2	0	1		4	4 Robbie Gardner	2*	1	0	2	R		1
5 Phil Bass	0	1*	2	2		5	5 Steve Finch	3	R	T	1	F	2	0
6 Steve Holden	2*	1	1			4	6 Phil Collins	1	0	1	T			0
7 Roy Sizmore	3	2	2*			7	7 Louis Carr	0	0	N				0
						47								30

Ht 01: Handley, Askew, Jackson (f), Smitherman (f)   68.1   5 - 0

Ht 02: Sizmore, Holden, Collins, Carr   67.4   10 - 1

Ht 03: Finch, Gardner, Wells, Bass   68.6   11 - 6

Ht 04: Leonard, Jackson, Holden, Carr   67.2   15 - 8

Ht 05: Jackson, Wells, Bass, Finch (ret)   68.2   18 - 11

Ht 06: Askew, Handley, Gardner, Collins   66.4   23 - 12

Ht 07: Leonard, Jackson, Holden, Gardner   66.5   27 - 14

Ht 08: Smitherman, Sizmore, Collins, Handley (f exc)   68.5   29 - 18

Ht 09: Smitherman, Bass, Finch, Wells   68.3   31 - 22

Ht 10: Askew, Gardner, Handley, Finch (f exc)   68.8   35 - 24

Ht 11: Leonard, Sizmore, Jackson, Smitherman   67.1   40 - 25

Ht 12: Askew, Finch, Wells, Smitherman   67.7   44 - 27

Ht 13: Jackson, Bass, Leonard, Gardner (ret)   68.2   47 - 30

CRAYFORD KESTRELS v OXFORD CHEETAHS

28ᵗʰ September 1976

49-27

(National League)

Team Manager (Kestrels): Peter Thorogood   Team Manager: Roger Jones

RIDERS INDIVIDUAL SCORE CHART													
CRAYFORD	1	2	3	4	5	T	OXFORD	1	2	3	4	5	T
1 Laurie Etheridge	3	3	3	3		12	1 Carl Askew	X	3	F	2	1	6
2 Richard Davey	F	0	2	2*		4	2 Mick Handley						RR
3 Alan Sage	2	3	3	3		11	3 Brian Leonard	3	2	0	1*	1	7
4 Mike Broadbank	2*	1*	2*	2*		7	4 Phil Bass	0	2	F	0		2
5 Alan Johns	3	2	3	2*		10	5 Jim Wells	1	1*	T	0		2
6 John Hooper	1*	1*	0			2	6 Roy Sizmore	3	0	1*	3	1	8
7 Gary Spencer	2	1*	0			3	7 Steve Holden	2	R	F	0		2
						49							27

Ht 01: Etheridge, Holden, Davey (f), Askew (exc)   62.4   3 - 2

Ht 02: Sizmore, Spencer, Hooper, Holden (ret)   62.6   6 - 5

Ht 03: Johns, Broadbank, Wells, Bass   63.2   11 - 6

Ht 04: Leonard, Sage, Hooper, Holden (f exc)   60.2   14 - 9

Ht 05: Askew, Johns, Broadbank, Sizmore   61.6   17 -12

Ht 06: Etheridge, Leonard, Sizmore, Davey   60.6   20 -15

Ht 07: Sage, Bass, Wells, Hooper   61.2   23 -18

Ht 08: Sizmore, Davey, Spencer, Holden   62.6   26 -21

Ht 09: Johns, Broadbank, Sizmore, Leonard   62.6   31 -22

Ht 10: Etheridge, Davey, Askew (f exc), Bass (f exc)   63.6   36 -22

Ht 11: Sage, Askew, Leonard, Spencer   60.8   39 -25

Ht 12: Etheridge, Broadbank, Leonard, Wells   62.2   44 -26

Ht 13: Sage, Johns, Askew, Bass   61.8   49 -27

Oxford v Canterbury v Crayford   30ᵗʰ September 1976

(Three Team Tournament) postponed due to rain

EASTBOURNE EAGLES v OXFORD CHEETAHS

3rd October 1976

49-29

(National League)

Team Manager (Eagles): Arthur Nutley   Team Manager: Roger Jones

RIDERS INDIVIDUAL SCORE CHART														
EASTBOURNE	1	2	3	4	5	T	OXFORD	1	2	3	4	5	6	T
1 Steve Weatherley	2*	2*	3	3		10	1 Brian Leonard	0	3	3	1	2	2	11
2 Eric Dugard	3	3	2*	0		8	2 Mick Handley							RR
3 Mike Sampson	3	1*	3	1		8	3 Carl Askew	X	0	0	1	N		1
4 Colin Richardson	E	1*	2	2*		5	4 Phil Bass	1	3	0	0	2	0	6
5 Pete Jarman	23	2	0	N		4	5 Jim Wells	1	T	X	1			2
6 Roger Abel	1	1	N			2	6 Roy Sizmore	2	2	1	3	0		8
7 Ian Gledhill	3	2	3	1	3	12	7 Steve Holden	0	0	T	1*			1
							8 Pip Lamb	0						0
						49								29

Ht 01: Dugard, Weatherley, Bass, Leonard   62.8   5 - 1

Ht 02: Gledhill, Sizmore, Abel, Holden   63.2   9 -3

Ht 03: Bass, Jarman, Wells, Richardson (ef)   63.4   11 - 7

Ht 04: Sampson, Sizmore, Abel, Holden, Askew (ex tapes)   63.2   15 - 9

Ht 05: Leonard, Jarman, Richardson, Bass (f rem)   61.8   18 -12

Ht 06: Dugard, Weatherley, Sizmore, Askew   63.4   23 -12

Ht 07: Leonard, Gledhill, Sampson, Bass   64.4   26 -16

Ht 08: Gledhill, Dugard, Leonard, Askew   65.0   31 -17

Ht 09: Sizmore, Richardson, Askew, Jarman   65.6   33 -21

Ht 10: Weatherley, Bass, Holden, Dugard, Wells (ex tapes)   63.6   36 -24

Ht 11: Sampson, Leonard, Gledhill, Sizmore   65.6   40 -26

Ht 12: Weatherley, Richardson, Wells, Lamb   65.2   45 -27

Ht 13: Gledhill, Leonard, Sampson, Bass   65.4   49 -29

OXFORD v CANTERBURY v CRAYFORD

7th October 1976

(Three Team Tournament)

Team Manager: Roger Jones

OXFORD	1	2	3	4	T
1 Brian Leonard	3	2	2*	2*	9
2 Kevin Young	2*	1*	3	3	9
3 Carl Askew	3	3	2*	3	11
4 Jim Wells	1	1	3	1	6
5 Phil Bass	1*	1*	3	2	7
6					
7 Colin Meredith	2	2	2*	1*	7
					49

Team Manager:

CANTERBURY	1	2	3	4	T
1 Les Rumsey	0	3	R	2	5
2 Barney Kennett	1	2*	2	R	5
3 Steve Koppe	3	3	1	2	9
4 Alan Diprose	0	0	0	1*	1
5 Graham Clifton	3	2*	1	3	9
6 Bob Spelta	0	3	F	N	3
7 Pip Lamb (G)	0				0
					32

Team Manager: Peter Thorogood

CRAYFORD	1	2	3	4	T
1 Laurie Etheridge	2	3	3	3	11
2 Gary Spencer	0	0	1	0	1
3 Alan Sage	2	2	2	3	9
4 Mike Bessent	1*	0	1*	N	2
5 Alan Johns	1	0	1	1	3
6 Mike Broadbank	0	1	0	0	1
7 Keith Pilcher(G)	0				0
					27

OXFORD v CANTERBURY v CRAYFORD   7th October 1976

Ht 01: Leonard, Young, Kennett, Rumsey   68.05

Ht 02: Koppe, Sage, Bessent, Diprose   69.80

Ht 03: Askew, Etheridge, Wells, Spencer   68.14

Ht 04: Clifton, Meredith, Bass, Spelta   68.23

Ht 05: Rumsey, Kennett, Johns, Broadbank   69.00

Ht 06: Etheridge, Leonard, Young, Spencer   67.03

Ht 07: Koppe, Meredith, Bass, Diprose   67.53

Ht 08: Spelta, Clifton, Broadbank, Johns   68.60

Ht 09: Askew, Sage, Wells, Bessent   67.44

Ht 10: Young, Leonard, Clifton, Spelta (f exc)   68.45

Ht 11: Etheridge, Kennett, Spencer, Rumsey (ret)   68.40

Ht 12: Bass, Meredith, Johns, Broadbank   68.25

Ht 13: Wells, Askew, Koppe, Diprose   68.85

Ht 14: Clifton, Sage, Bessent, Lamb   67.50

Ht 15: Young, Leonard, Johns, Broadbank   68.25

Ht 16: Askew, Rumsey, Wells, Kennett (ret)   68.24

Ht 17: Etheridge, Koppe, Diprose, Spencer   69.20

Ht 18: Sage, Bass, Meredith, Pilcher   68.13

Mike Broadbank 2017

HARTFORD MOTORS SUPER NATIONAL

Sunday 31st October 1976, 15.30

This meeting owes much to Pete Cundy, who organised sponsorship throughout the season with his employer, Hartford Motors. The fans were offered opportunities to sponsor heats and present a prize to the heat winner, which went down extremely well.

The first prize was a Weslake engine, costing around £500, to be presented by Harry Weslake.

HARTFORD MOTORS SUPER NATIONAL

Each heat was individually sponsored

Heat 1 OXFORD SPEEDWAY SUPPORTERS CLUB	**Heat 8** MAXIMUM RACING Landford, Salisbury	**Heat 15** SOS COMMITTEE
Heat 2 BRISTOL SPEEDWAY SUPPORTERS CLUB	**Heat 9** THE FOREMAN Mick Harris, SOS	**Heat 16** PEGASUS SPEED-NEEDS Baddelsey, Hants
Heat 3 MORETON MOTORS Grasstrack and Speedway Supplies	**Heat 10** CRAVEN MOTORS B. Leonard. Thatcham	**Heat 17** OXFORD STADIUM CLUB
Heat 4 MORETON MOTORS Sieger – Hagon - Briggo	**Heat 11** LESANDON DRUG STORES	**Heat 18** I. JONES & SON Livestock Transport
Heat 5 MORETON MOTORS Leathers, helmets, tyres, tubes	**Heat 12** St JOHN AMBULANCE	**Heat 19** TAPPINS COACHES Didcot
Heat 6 JOHN BARNEY & SONS Plant Hire, Demolition	**Heat 13** ART DEANS Honda Motor Cycles	**Heat 20** DYNAMITE ROAD SHOW Good Record Selection
Heat 7 MAXIMUM RACING Speedway Products	**Heat 14** ART DEANS Motorcycles, Scooters	**Heat 21** HARTFORD MOTORS

CONSOLATION PRIZES

GROVE PRODUCTS - "Hard Luck Cheetah – Bike Cover

KEITH LAWSON & JOHN HALL (Photographers) – "Lucky Dip" - Fruit Basket

HARRY & TONY (Promoters) - "Mr Unlucky" - Bottle of Scotch

Les Collins and Martin Yeates in the pits

Riders		1	2	3	4	5	Pts	Pos
01 Colin Richardson	(Eastbourne)	2	2	2	2	2	10	3rd
02 Bob Garrad	(Rye House)	0	3	0	2	1	6	9th
03 Les Collins	(Stoke)	3	3	3	2	3	14	1st
04 Martin Yeates	(Weymouth)	1	1	2	1	2	7	6th
05 Brian Clark	(Peterborough)	1	1	3	1	0	6	10th
06 Steve Koppe	(Canterbury)	2	2	0	3	1	8	5th
07 Alan Sage	(Crayford)	3	1	F	3	E	7	7th
08 David Ashby	(Swindon)	0	2	0	3	1	6	11th
09 Roy Sizmore	(Oxford)	1	0	2	0	2	5	15th
10 Ted Hubbard	(Rye House)	3	0	3	3	3	12	2nd
11 Brian Leonard	(Oxford)	2	0	1	0	3	6	12th
12 Kevin Young	(Oxford)	0	3	1	0	2	6	13th
13 Eric Dugard	(Eastbourne)	0	3	1	1	0	5	16th
14 Steve Weatherley	(Eastbourne)	2	1	1	1	1	6	14th
15 Laurie Etheridge	(Crayford)	1	2	2	2	0	7	8th
16 Colin Meredith	(Oxford)	3	0	3	F	3	9	4th

Ht 01: Collins, Richardson, Yeates, Garrad   65.8

Ht 02: Sage, Koppe, Clark, Ashby   68.0

Ht 03: Hubbard, Leonard, Sizmore, Young   67.2

Ht 04: Meredith, Weatherley, Etheridge, Dugard   64.8

Ht 05: Dugard, Richardson, Clark, Sizmore   67.4

Ht 06: Garrad, Koppe, Weatherley, Hubbard   66.7

Ht 07: Collins, Etheridge, Sage, Leonard   67.0

Ht 08: Young, Ashby, Yeates, Meredith (f rem)   67.1

Ht 09: Meredith, Richardson, Leonard, Koppe   66.0

Ht 10: Clark, Etheridge, Young, Garrad   67.7

Ht 11: Collins, Sizmore, Weatherley, Ashby   68.2

Ht 12: Hubbard, Yeates, Dugard, Sage (f exc)   68.5

Ht 13: Sage, Richardson, Weatherley, Young   66.8

Ht 14: Ashby, Garrad, Dugard, Leonard   66.7

Ht 15: Hubbard, Collins, Clark, Meredith (f)   67.6

Ht 16: Koppe, Etheridge, Yeates, Sizmore   68.9

Ht 17: Hubbard, Richardson, Ashby, Etheridge   67.0

Ht 18: Meredith, Sizmore, Garrad, Sage (ef)   69.0

Ht 19: Collins, Young, Koppe, Dugard   68.1

Ht 20: Leonard, Yeates, Weatherley, Clark   68.3

Heat 1: Martin Yeates leads Les Collins

HARTFORD MOTORS SUPER NATIONAL

Heat 2: David Ashby, Steve Koppe, Brian Clark, Alan Sage

Heat 2: Alan Sage and Brian Clark

Heat 2: David Ashby

HARTFORD MOTORS SUPER NATIONAL

Heat 3: Kevin Young, Roy Sizmore, Brian Leonard, Ted Hubbard

Heat 3: Ted Hubbard

Heat 3:Ted Hubbard and Brian Leonard

HARTFORD MOTORS SUPER NATIONAL

Heat 4: Colin Meredith, Eric Dugard

Heat 4: Colin Meredith

Heat 4: Colin Meredith

HARTFORD MOTORS SUPER NATIONAL

Heat 5: Colin Richardson

Heat 5: Eric Dugard

Heat 5: Roy Sizmore

HARTFORD MOTORS SUPER NATIONAL

Heat 6: Bob Garrad (I think)

Heat 8: Kevin Young

Heat 11: Les Collins receives his prize from Les Windle

Heat 12: Ted Hubbard wins the St John's sponsored heat (Supt Bill Tombs)

HARTFORD MOTORS SUPER NATIONAL

Heat 17: Ted Hubbard receives his prize from Tony West

Heat 18: Colin Meredith receives his prize from Roger Jones

Ted Hubbard receives his prize from Keith Lawson (ME!)
photo by John Hall on my camera

HARTFORD MOTORS SUPER NATIONAL

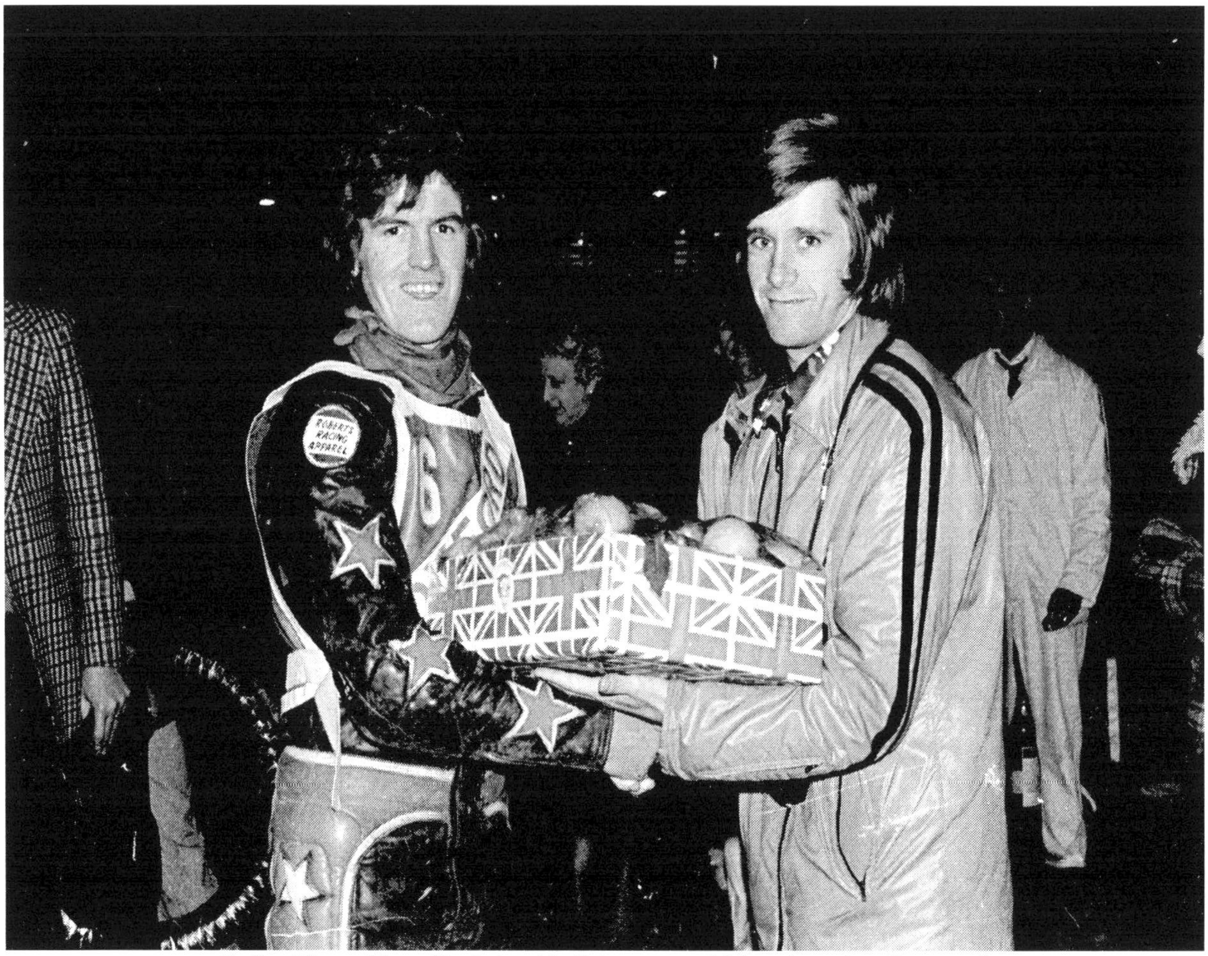

Colin Meredith with John Hall (my good friend and colleague)

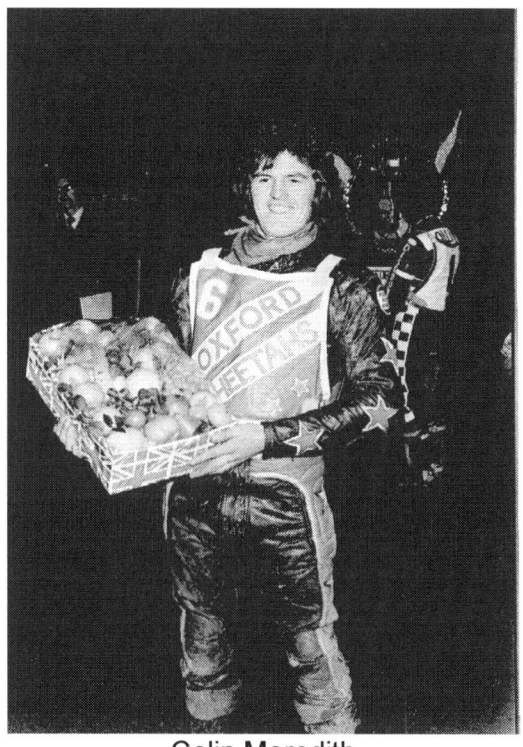

Colin Meredith

HARTFORD MOTORS SUPER NATIONAL

Ted Hubbard with Glynn Shailes

Harry Bastable, Les Collins, and Tony Allsopp

Pete Cundy, Harry Weslake, Les Collins, Mrs Weslake

Pete Cundy and Les Collins

PHOTOS FOR THE ALBUM

The "victory" ride, on the tractor

Harry MacLean

Pip Lamb receives the
George Squires cup

Final National League Table For 1976

	Teams	P	W	D	L	F	A	Pts
1	Newcastle	34	30	1	3	1642	1007	61
2	Ellesmere Port	34	24	1	9	1446.5	1196.5	49
3	Workington	34	20	1	13	1405.5	1235.5	41
4	Canterbury	34	20	0	14	1344	1302	40
5	Rye House	34	17	2	15	1357.5	1205.5	36
6	Crayford	34	17	1	16	1354	1286	35
7	Coatbridge	34	17	1	16	1316	1320	35
8	Eastbourne	34	17	0	17	1361	1281	34
9	Peterborough	34	16	2	16	1351	1260	34
10	Berwick	34	17	0	17	1278	1360	34
11	Stoke	34	15	1	18	1304	1340	31
12	Boston	34	15	1	18	1298	1345	31
13	Mildenhall	34	15	1	18	1270	1378	31
14	**Oxford**	**34**	**14**	**1**	**19**	**1257**	**1350**	**239**
15	Weymouth	34	11	2	21	1186.5	1454.5	24
16	Paisley	34	12	0	22	1152	1492	24
17	Scunthorpe	34	11	1	22	1184	1379	23
18	Teeside	34	10	0	24	1163	1478	20

Phil Bass with a young fan picked from the crowd to present a tankard

Mick Handley and Pete Cundy

Kevin Young and Pete Cundy

Oxford Cheetahs with Pete Cundy

Carl Askew and Bernard Crapper

Steve Windle - Mascot

Apologies for the quality of these photos (originals are colour)

ACKNOWLEDGEMENTS

Thanks to the following

For the data on match results for the season

Steve Wilkes and Gary Done.

Their diligence in compiling the statistics has been invaluable in the creation of this book and the first in the series "The Rebels 1975", which details the last season of the Rebels at Oxford.

For researching and supplying names I was struggling to source – **Steve Roberts**

All the photos are mine bar 1 (John Hall) –

(Google keith lawson speedway) to see extensive use of my work.

See my modern work at https://l4w50n.wixsite.com/sppaonline

All clipart is believed to be royalty-free, from various sources.

While all the photos in the book are monochrome, some originals were in colour and they can be seen on-line on Facebook "The Home of Oxford Cheetahs Speedway"

https://www.facebook.com/groups/271522546314436/   (c) 2018 Keith Lawson

IN MEMORIAM

Those Cheetahs (riders, staff and supporters) we have lost along the way

PHIL BASS	BERNARD CRAPPER
PETE JARMAN	PETE CUNDY
STEVE HOLDEN	GEORGE SQUIRES
GEORGE HUNTER	NORMAN HUNTER
ASHLEY PULLEN	BOB RADFORD
SIMON WIGG	

and, on behalf of all Oxford fans

Danny Dunton

Bob Dugard

I cannot guarantee the accuracy of data or the identification of photos, whether the right rider named or it being the match claimed, but I have tried my hardest.
I have attempted to correct spelling of names from programmes (where the promoters got them wrong) but mistakes might still have got through.

No apologies for including poorer quality photos than would normally be seen in publications – my reason is, that whatever the quality, it is part of the record of 1976.

Keith Lawson 2018

If you've enjoyed this pictorial history of Oxford speedway, why not get this companion book?

Rebels 1975 - The Last Season

By Keith Lawson

View this Author's Spotlight

Paperback, 180 Pages ☆☆☆☆☆   This item has not been rated yet

Preview

Prints in 3-5 business days

A unique collection of over 300 photos recalling the final year of Oxford Rebels (1975) - the riders, the races, the champions. With references and photos of all the British League teams that year. Plus the results of the matches with individual riders' scores.

The photo history with match results and riders' scores of the last season of Oxford Rebels.

Available direct from the printer (www.lulu.com/shop)

[look for frequent discount offer codes on the website before ordering]

Printed in Great Britain
by Amazon